FINANCIAL
SIGNIFICATORS
in Traditional Astrology

Öner Döşer, AMA, ISAR CAP

Edited with a Preface by
BENJAMIN N. DYKES, PHD

The Cazimi Press
Minneapolis, Minnesota
2018

Published and printed in the United States of America

First American edition published by:
The Cazimi Press
Minneapolis, MN

Translation by:
Sibel Oltulu

Edited by:
Mustafa Konur, Sibel Oltulu, and Benjamin N. Dykes

Original design by:
Mustafa Konur
mustafakonur@gmail.com

AstroArt Astroloji ve Danışmanlık Ltd. Şti.
Bağdat Cad. No. 284 Canoğlu Apt.
Kat: 3 Daire: 20 Kadıköy/İstanbul
Tel: 0216 386 73 96
www.astrolojiokulu.com
info@astrolojiokulu.com
Certificate No: 22202

ISBN-13: 978-1-934586-46-4

TABLE OF CONTENTS

This book is part of a new series in support of the traditional astrology courses of the AstroArt Astrology School in Istanbul, headed by my friend and colleague Öner Döşer. It follows our successful 2015 release of his popular *Astrological Prediction: A Handbook of Techniques* (2015).

After a long career in Istanbul's oldest and most prestigious bazaar, Öner followed his heart and turned fully to astrology, soon becoming one of the leading astrologers in Turkey, with numerous television appearances and books to his credit. His Astrology School Publishing has released 14 well-received books, not to mention his own articles in international astrological publications. Since 2012 he has been the organizer of the highly successful International Astrology Days in Istanbul.

Öner Döşer's blends traditional and modern techniques and attitudes. For example, for the most part he uses Placidus houses, but for certain techniques he focuses on whole signs. In terms of planets, he uses the three outers as well as Chiron. However, he grounds his work in traditional authors, such as Ptolemy, Dorotheus, Firmicus Maternus, Māshā'allāh, Sahl, Abū Ma'shar, Schoener, Lilly, and others. For this new series I have largely provided my own translations of the source material (both current and forthcoming), with sentence numbers in boldface in the footnotes. In some cases, I have updated older translations to reflect my current thinking. I have also added a few comments of my own, prefaced with **BD**.

I know you will enjoy these succinct and helpful guides to astrological interpretation, and your chart reading will improve as a result.

Benjamin Dykes, 2018

INTRODUCTION

The significators in a natal chart do not only signify the native's personal characteristics and psychological profile. Within a chart there are many significators which signify the native's health, money, profession, children, other people in his life, and many other things. These crucial significators may be determined through certain special techniques, and help us make more precise and detailed predictions regarding the native's life.

The issues that attract the attention of contemporary astrologers seem to differ from those of the ancient astrologers. The greatest difference between traditional and contemporary astrology is that traditionally the planets in a chart are not only attributed to the native, but also to other people signified through these planets. Traditional astrology is based on distinguishing and determining the planets which signify different issues.

First of all, we need to consider what a significator represents by its nature. According to traditional astrologers, the Sun represents the native's father in particular, but also all male figures who are authoritative in the native's life. The Moon signifies the native's mother in particular, but is also the general significator of female figures. She is also considered when determining the native's health problems. Mercury is related generally to all siblings, whereas Mars is related to brothers especially. The native's mind is busy in the matters of the house where Mercury is located, and this house indicates where we use our talents. We are faced with challenges, hatred, and aggression in the house where Mars is located. Venus represents young women, wives, and also young sisters. We find joy and pleasure where Venus is located in the chart. Jupiter and Saturn represent wisdom. Jupiter is also related to wealthy people, financial wealth, where ease and freedom is, and also genuine feelings and sincerity. In nocturnal charts Saturn represents the father and grandfathers, poor people, and hard work. There is fear where Saturn is located in the chart.

These significators are interpreted through the houses they are located in, as well as their zodiacal positions, to delineate the people and issues they are attributed to. For example, the location of Venus, the houses she rules, and her aspects, give us information about the people and events delineated by this planet. Let's assume Venus is in the 12th house: we may interpret that the native's sister is his secret enemy. Let's assume Venus is also burned and squares Saturn: so, this sister may be ill or fighting against difficulties.

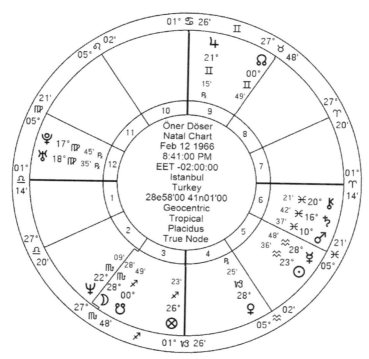

Figure 1: Öner Döşer

Let's think of a chart with Venus in the 4th house. As Venus is physically placed here, she is the accidental significator of the 4th house.

So, she shapes the issues of the 4th house according to her own nature, which helps us predict events related to the 4th. In addition, Venus brings her Venusian nature to bear on the 4th, by means of the houses she rules. Let's assume Venus is the domicile lord of the 1st, 2nd, and 9th houses, and the exaltation lord of the 6th. As she is located in the 4th, she links the issues of these houses to the 4th.

If there is more than one planet in a house, each planet shows its impact in its own time, starting with the planet which is closest to the house cusp. For example, let's assume that Mars, the Sun, and Mercury are in the 11th house, and Mars is the closest one to the house cusp. If the other planets in this house (the Sun and Mercury), do not rule this house (that is, if they are not the domicile or exaltation lords, or the victor), then Mars will dominate the events related to this house. This means Mars is the accidental significator of the matters related to the 11th house. The native's friends, social environment, income earned from his profession, his hopes and expectations, are all ruled by Mars. The issues related to the other houses ruled by Mars will automatically be linked to the issues of the 11th. Let's remember our golden rule: being physically present in a house is superior to what a planet signifies by its rulership of other houses.

In the example chart below (Figure 2) which belongs to my dear teacher Robert Zoller, since Mars is both physically present in this house and one of the lords of this house (as exaltation lord and victor), and also the nearest planet to the house cusp, he is the accidental significator of issues related to the 11th house. It means that the people and events represented by the 11th are of a Martial nature: disagreeable, conflicting, competitive, aggressive, irritated, ambitious, leaders, brave, direct, unreliable, etc. If Venus were the significator of the 11th house, then the native's friends would be Venusian types: pretty, moderate, compatible, elegant, cheerful, and playful.

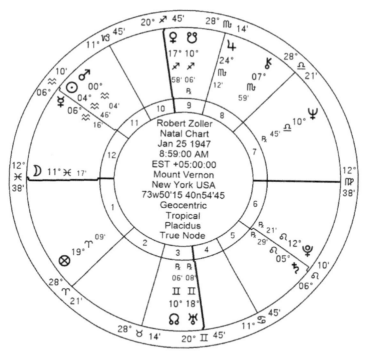

Figure 2: Robert Zoller

When making a judgment, we should also consider the aspects of the significator in addition to its house location and rulerships. In our example Mars, the significator of the 11ᵗʰ house, is in conjunction with the Sun and Mercury, and in opposition with Saturn. We may judge that the native has competitive and conflicting relations with his friends. There may be a leadership struggle among them. The native's friends are Martian types. As Mars is in Aquarius and rules the 9ᵗʰ house, his friends may have radical ideas and original ideologies. They may also be interested in the sciences and astrology as well. As Mars rules the 9ᵗʰ house of this chart, the native's friends may be foreigners, people from academia, or involved in other 9ᵗʰ house issues, or his friends may encourage him in investments because Mars is the lord of the 2ⁿᵈ house and the Lot of Fortune. Perhaps the native will earn money through some organization or group. The native's friends may be involved in secret affairs, or ill, or have some losses, because Mars is burned and in opposition with Saturn (Saturn also rules the 12th house). The native's friends may be his partners because Mars conjoins with Mercury. His reputation may be in danger due to his friends and social circles. His friends may cause his bad reputation because the Sun is afflicted by Mars and Saturn: Mars as the significator of the 11th house, and Saturn as the domicile lord of the 11th, represent the native's friends and social groups.

Moreover, there are other significators specific to a topic. Although they differ in each chart, they signify certain issues like marriage, children, finances, profession, the religious life, etc. By preparing a table of victors as suggested by traditional astrologers (see Appendix B), we may determine the dignities of the significators. The zodiacal state of the significator (the sign and house it is in, its aspects, the state of its lord) help us determine the course of the topic we are dealing with. For example, for the issues related to marriage we need to find the Marriage Victor. So, we need the zodiacal degrees of the significators related to marriage, which are:

1. The cusp of the 7th house.
2. The lord of the 7th house.
3. Venus.
4. The Lot of marriage and its lord.
5. The first triplicity lord of the 7th house.

If the victor over these significators are harmoniously configured with the lord of the Ascendant, then the native has a harmonious marriage—whereas their incompatibility indicates a negative course of marriage. If these significators (or the strongest one of them) is in angular or succeedent houses, if they are not in contact with the malefics, not burned, retrograde, or in cadent houses, and if they are in contact with the lord of the Ascendant, then the marriage will be a good and proper one. (See Appendix B for how to calculate a victor.)

The purpose of this book

In this book I will describe how traditional astrologers determined the financial significator and how they used all of the significators in judgments, providing some examples so that astrology students may easily understand these techniques. My primary purpose is to introduce these methodical and reliable techniques to contemporary astrologers.

My own specialty is in the medieval period of the Art of astrology, but through other references (in addition to those from my dear teacher and master Robert Zoller), I also aim to introduce you to the rules and techniques used by the ancient astrologers. In addition to this book on financial significators, you may also want to explore my books on other important significators. I believe that astrology students who modestly and diligently practice these methods and rules of the older masters, will easily determine the significators in a chart and make correct interpretations.

I hope this book reminds students of astrology that the traditional techniques are methodical and efficient, and help restore the inextricable link between today's astrology and its traditional origins.

Öner Döşer
Astroart School of Astrology, ASA, Istanbul, Turkey
http://www.astrolojiokulu.com/en

1: FINANCIAL SIGNIFICATORS

In a birth chart, it is possible to find out what matters the native may profit from and how, and alternative ways of making money. As we do when determining other significators in the chart, we will find the financial significator by identifying the possible significators and choosing the strongest among them. To find the significator we will look at the methods suggested by ancient astrologers, beginning with Claudius Ptolemy (from the classical period) up to William Lilly, a late Renaissance astrologer. Then we will find our own method through a synthesis of all we have learned from the ancients.

Modern astrologers consider the sign on the cusp of the 2nd house, the planet(s) located in the 2nd, and the lord of this house when determining the financial significator. Traditional astrologers consider some additional significators for finding out how the native will earn money and where his general welfare comes from: these are the Lot of Fortune, the Lot of assets, and Jupiter. Additionally, the Sun in a diurnal chart, the Moon in a nocturnal chart, and their triplicity lords are also considered. The lord of the Ascendant is also one of the significators. Now, let's get into some details and see what the authorities from the traditional period said about this topic.

The Lot of Fortune, as we are also familiar with from the modern period, is considered as the sole significator of the native's good fortune deriving from wealth in Ptolemy's *Tetrabiblos*. He says: "What the subject's material acquisitions will be, is to be gained from the so-called 'Lot of Fortune.'"[1]

Ptolemy calculates the Lot of Fortune using only the diurnal formula given below, whereas all other astrologers say there

---

[1] *Tet.* IV.2 (Robbins p. 373).

should be different formulas for day and night. In his book *The Arabic Parts*, Zoller also says that the nocturnal formula should be used in nocturnal charts.[2] I agree with this opinion. Here is the formula:

Diurnal: Ascendant + Moon – Sun.
Nocturnal: Ascendant + Sun – Moon.

Ptolemy suggests that after finding this Lot, its lord's position should be considered. If its lord is favorably placed and supported by the luminaries, then the financial situation of the native is good. Ptolemy also recommends we consider its aspects with other planets, in this short chapter (Ch. IV.2).

According to **Firmicus Maternus**, "From this place is shown the quality of life, the assets[3] of the patrimony, and the course of luckiness and unluckiness; even how the love and affection of men concerning women is, is learned from this place, and the bringing about of all nourishment[4] and desires is sought from the essence of this place."[5]

Unlike Ptolemy, Firmicus—who calculates the Lot differently for diurnal and nocturnal charts—suggests we make our evaluation based on the house it is located in, its position in zodiac, and its aspects. In the next step, Firmicus says we should consider if the Lot aspects the Moon in a nocturnal chart or the Sun in a diurnal chart. Then he says: "But if the lord of all of these portions[6] was found to be one [and the same planet] and it is placed well in

---

[2] Zoller 1989, p. 85.
[3] **BD**: Or, "essence" (*substantia*).
[4] This particularly pertains to early upbringing in general, which largely concerns the care and health of a young child's body.
[5] *Mathesis* IV.17, **9-10**.
[6] **BD**: That is, "degrees" (of the Sun by day, or the Moon by night). Often when Firmicus uses this phrase he means the lord of the bounds, but it would also make sense to find the victor over the luminary using all the dignities.

the birth, and in these signs in which it rejoices or in which it is exalted or in which it is the lord, it decrees a lucky birth. But if it was placed together with the Sun or Moon *and* regarded the place of Fortune, a greater, manifold luckiness is decreed through the raying."[7]

This statement potentially identifies two planets: the first is the the one with the highest rank among those having dignities in the degrees of the Sun and the Moon; and the second is the one which aspects the luminary of the sect (and ideally Fortune as well). In any case, the position of this planet in the chart and its aspect with the Lot of Fortune is important. According to Firmicus, the Lot of Fortune in one of the angular houses, having an aspect with the Moon, points out a luckier chart.[8]

'Umar al-Tabarī says, "If you wished to look in the matter of assets, look at the second from the Ascendant and whatever of the planets is in it, and at the lord of the second, and at the Lot of assets and the lord of the Lot, also at Jupiter, and the Lot of Fortune and its lord. Then look at the victor over these places, whether it was one or two."[9] So, 'Umar states that the following elements should be considered in determining the native's income:

Planets located in the 2nd house.
The lord of the 2nd.
The Lot of Fortune and its lord.
The Lot of assets and its lord.
Jupiter.

---

[7] *Mathesis* IV.17, **12-13**. **BD**: This could also be read as, "a greater luckiness is decreed by the manifold raying." In Firmicus, "raying" is a degree-based aspect, and he generally has exact or very close ones in mind (rather than just by sign).
[8] *Mathesis* IV.17, **14**.
[9] Al-Tabarī, *TBN* III.2 (p. 52).

Next, the victor over these significators should be determined.[10] This planet is the one which best reflects the native's financial situation. The relationship between this planet and the lord of the Ascendant should also be evaluated. In this way we can determine how much the native may earn. The position of the victor is also used to determine in which period of life the native will make profit: if the victor is eastern, he makes profit at earlier ages; if it is western, he makes profit at later ages. The triplicity lords of the victor also indicate the native's profits in their respective periods of life.

According to **Abu 'Ali al-Khayyāt**, "Look at the 2nd house from the Ascendant: which if fortunes were in it or aspected, and the bad ones were not in it nor aspected, and its lord [was] in a good place in the circle and relative to the Sun, they will signify fortune, and the native's success in readying resources. But if on the other hand they bore themselves in a converse manner, they portend detriment for the native in matters of assets."[11]

Next, the aspect between the lord of the Ascendant and the lord of the 2nd house should be considered. Here applying and separating aspects gain importance. According to Abu 'Ali,[12] if the lord of the 2nd house applies to the lord of the Ascendant, it signifies the acquisition of much money without any hard work because money already flows to the native. However, if conversely the lord of the Ascendant applies to the lord of the 2nd, it signifies an increase in assets but with hard work. If this aspect comes from an angular house, it signifies much wealth arising from things already known. But if the application is from a succeedent house, than the native's gains will be fine but less.

If there is no aspect between the lord of the Ascendant and the lord of the 2nd, then only the lord of the 2nd should be considered.

---

[10] Al-Tabarī, *TBN* III.2 (p. 52).
[11] Al-Khayyāt, *JN* Ch. 11 (p. 261).
[12] Al-Khayyāt, *JN* Ch. 11 (p. 261).

If it is in one of the angular houses and not afflicted by the malefics, or if the Moon is in a similar position in a nocturnal chart,[13] then the native earns well. However, if the lord of the 2nd is one of the cadent houses, and especially if afflicted by the malefics, then the native has difficulties in earning money to satisfy his needs.

The contact between the lord of the Ascendant and Jupiter should also be considered. If there is a contact between them it signifies prosperity, especially if reception also accompanies the application.[14]

Then,[15] the Lot of Fortune and its lord should be considered. If they are favorably placed, secure from the hard aspects of malefics (not in conjunction, square or opposition with them) and if they are in aspect with the Ascendant, then it signifies good profit and good luck.

If[16] the lord of the Lot of Fortune or the Lot of assets is burned, it signifies some bad conditions and a decrease in the native's gains.

If[17] the Lot of Fortune is in conjunction, square, or opposition with benefics and not afflicted by malefics, it signifies much benefit to the native and to his fortune. If the Lot is in conjunction, square, or opposition with malefics but not supported by benefics, then it signifies evil conditions for the native and little of anything good.

The[18] triplicity lords of the 2nd house should also be considered, because they also have signification in matters of wealth and each of them gives information about one-third of life, in accordance with their own nature and strength.

---

[13] **BD**: Al-Khayyāt does not specify the sect of the chart, but the Moon would be especially important in a nocturnal chart.
[14] Al-Khayyāt, *JN* Ch. 11 (p. 262).
[15] Al-Khayyāt, *JN* Ch. 11 (p. 262).
[16] Al-Khayyāt, *JN* Ch. 11 (p. 262).
[17] Al-Khayyāt, *JN* Ch. 11 (pp. 262-63).
[18] Al-Khayyāt, *JN* Ch. 11 (p. 262).

If[19] the triplicity lords of the 2nd house aspect the cusp of the 2nd, if benefics are located in the Ascendant or in the 2nd house, then it signifies benefit in terms of the native's wealth.

If[20] the Moon is received while aspecting the Ascendant, it signifies that the native will have much money and good circumstances, especially if the planet it receives is a fortune. The same is valid when the Moon is located in one of the angular or succeedent houses, waxing, and conjoining her management and power to a fortune, and to the planet receiving her.

If[21] the triplicity lords of the Sun in a diurnal chart (or the triplicity lords of the Moon in a nocturnal chart) are in contact with the lord of the Lot of Fortune, or the Lot of assets, or Jupiter, not afflicted and favorably placed in the chart, they signify wealth in accordance with their own nature and position. On the contrary if they are unfavorably placed, then the native will have difficulties and evil conditions.

Guido Bonatti suggests[22] that the Lot of Fortune and its lord, the Lot of assets and its lord, the planets located in the 2nd house, the sign on the cusp of the 2nd, the lord of the 2nd, and Jupiter, should be considered for the prosperity and assets of the native and his acquisitions. He claims that a financial significator should posses these qualities: it should not be afflicted (although in my experience being in fall is acceptable if there is no other affliction and its lord is in a good condition), at least one of its lords should make an aspect to it (but the nature of its aspect is not important), the lords of some significators should not be afflicted. The house

---

[19] **BD:** This sentence is not in al-Khayyāt, but it makes good astrological sense.

[20] Al-Khayyāt, *JN* Ch. 11 (p. 262). **BD:** The Latin al-Khayyāt has the last part of this somewhat garbled, so I have borrowed from the Arabic version in Sahl's *Nativities*, Ch. 2.13, **29**.

[21] Al-Khayyāt, *JN* Ch. 11 (p. 263).

[22] **BD:** The following summary can be found in Bonatti's Tr. IX.3, 2nd House Ch. 1, pp. 1,200-30.

where the significator is placed and the houses where its lords are placed, signify where the native will make money from.

According to Bonatti, we should follow a certain order when determining the financial significator. The aim here is to determine the ideal fields that the native may profit from, and to determine his earning power. Bonatti says that we should first consider the Lot of Fortune, and ensure that (1) the Lot is not afflicted, and (2) at least one of the lords of the Lot is making an aspect to it, and this lord is not afflicted. A lord in detriment is not in a position to support this Lot. If all the lords of the Lot are in detriment, then it is hard to expect the effects of this Lot to be big and permanent.

As I mentioned above, first of all we should consider whether or not the Lot is afflicted, and if at least one of its lords is in aspect with it. The one which aspects the Lot and which is the strongest should be preferred. It should not be afflicted. For example, if the lord of the Lot aspects it but the lord is afflicted, or if it does not aspect the Lot but is not afflicted, then the Lot should not be chosen as the significator. In that case we should skip to the exalted lord, and then the other lords in turn. If the lords do not make aspects with the Lot, even if they are not afflicted, then the Lot of Fortune is not considered the financial significator.

If the Lot of Fortune cannot be the financial significator, then we may consider the Lot of assets. We apply the same rules as above for the Lot of assets. The formula is:

Ascendant + Cusp of 2nd - lord of 2nd (both night and day)

If none of the lords of the Lot aspect it, or if the lords aspect the Lot but they are afflicted, we should skip to the next possible financial significator.

In the next step, the lord of the 2nd house and planets located in the 2nd should be considered. Again, the above procedure should be followed; domicile and exaltation lords should be considered first of all. The other lords are less likely to be the financial significator. We should consider their aspects with the cusp of the 2nd house, but that may not be a suitable option because these aspects may change when other house systems are used. Whether or not the lord of the 2nd is the financial significator, its planetary nature and the house it is located in, will indicate something of where the earnings of the native come from.

If one of the lords of the 2nd house cannot be the financial significator, then we should consider Jupiter, which is the general significator of wealth. Jupiter may be the financial significator if he is not afflicted. There is no rule requiring that Jupiter should make an aspect with one of his lords. Basically, if there is no financial significator, we may expect profit from the fields where Jupiter is involved.

If[23] Jupiter cannot be the financial significator, then the luminaries are considered: the Sun in a diurnal chart and the Moon in a nocturnal chart. If the luminaries are not afflicted and are located in favorable houses, then they may be the financial significator.

If none of the luminaries may be the financial significator, then the victor or most dignified planet over the degrees of the Lot of Fortune and Lot of assets should be considered. If the planet which is determined as the victor in the degree of these two Lots is not afflicted, then it may be the financial significator.

If none of the above-mentioned significators is suited to be the financial significator, then the following elements should be considered respectively:

- Triplicity lords of 2nd house (if not afflicted, favorably located).
- Triplicity lords of sect light (if not afflicted, favorably located).
- Triplicity lords of Ascendant (if not afflicted, favorably located).

---

[23] Bonatti, Tr. IX.3, 2nd House, Ch. 1 (pp. 1,202-03).

According to Robert Zoller, if one of these significators is favorable but cannot be the financial significator according to the rules, then the native's earning capacity is very limited; he may even be poor.[24]

---

[24] Zoller, *Diploma* Lesson 13 (p. 11).

2: ANALYZING THE LOT OF FORTUNE

This Lot and its placement in the chart provide information about the luck, prosperity, success, and gains of the native. It is also associated with the Moon, which is why it also relates to the native's instincts: that is, it concerns the areas of life in which the native tries to realize his or her own desires and needs. The sign and house where the lord of the Lot is placed, tells us in which areas of life these needs and desires are realized, and in which way. Actually the Lot of Fortune is used in many chart topics, from the native's financial situation to the length of life, to the ruler of the chart as a whole. Even when the Lot is not the official significator of financial resources, its house location can be seen as a good luck indicator for income and financial gains.

According to Guido Bonatti, this Lot "signifies life, the body also, and its soul; strength and fortune and assets, and success. Also riches and poverty; even gold and silver; the expensiveness or cheapness of things bought in the marketplace; even praise and good reputation, and honors and loftiness, good and bad, what is present and what is to be, [whether] hidden or manifest. And it has a signification over every matter. However, it does more for the wealthy and for great men than for others; but for every man it also works according to the condition of each one of them. And if this Lot and the luminaries were well disposed in nativities or revolutions, there will be good in a notable way. And it is called the Lot of the Moon, and is the Ascendant of the Moon, and signifies good fortune."[25]

In traditional texts, we see that the Lot is considered fundamental in matters related to the native's gains and welfare. Ptolemy suggests we consider its lord after determining the place of the

---

[25] Bonatti, Tr. VIII.2, 2nd House, Ch.1 (p. 1,044-45).

Lot, because the native earns money through the professions indicated by this planet: "Thus Saturn brings riches through building, or agriculture, or shipping ventures, Jupiter through fiduciary relationships, guardianships, or priesthoods, Mars through military operations and command, Venus through gifts from friends or women, and Mercury through eloquence and trade."[26] Ptolemy also says we should consider the configurations of this lord with other planets.

In Dorotheus we may see some evaluations based on the aspects of the lord of the Lot of Fortune and its configurations with other planets. Let me quote a paragraph from his book: "And if you found the lord of the Lot made unfortunate but the fortunes in a good place, testifying to the Ascendant and the Moon, and the fortunes are eastern, then he will be middling in assets and livelihood. Because when Jupiter is in a good position he always indicates that the native will attain good from the nobility and the powerful ones of the people, and work and benefit, and he will acquire assets for that reason; and if Venus was <in> a place like that she indicates benefit because of females; and if Mercury were in that place, he indicates benefiting because of commerce, knowledge, and calculation; and if Mercury and Jupiter mixed together, he will be trusted among kings and groups."[27]

In addition to paying attention to the signs where the Lot and its lord are, I believe we should also make our evaluations based on the nature of the planets aspecting the Lot. In the next chapter you may find brief interpretations for aspects between the Lot of Fortune and the planets. These interpretations are also valid for the lords of the Lot, which means that the information under the title *Saturn-Lot of Fortune* is also valid when Saturn is the lord of the Lot of Fortune. Although I include the generational planets, in

---

[26] *Tet.* IV.2 (Robbins p. 375).
[27] *Carmen* I.28, **23-24**.

terms of rulerships only the traditional lords should be considered (like Mars for Scorpio, Saturn for Aquarius, and Jupiter for Pisces).

The Lot of Fortune's aspect or conjunction with planets indicates areas of life which the native's welfare and gains are related to. A native with favorable aspects to the Lot may seize opportunities easily, while a native with unfavorable aspects may not, may only have limited fortune, or may not even have any fortune because of the nature of the planets in aspect.

3: THE LOT OF FORTUNE AND THE PLANETS

Saturn - Lot of Fortune

The native needs to work hard, take responsibility, and make effort in order to obtain opportunities in life. He avoids taking risks in financial issues. He may not seize chances and use opportunities quickly. He cares about being financially secure, is anxious about financial issues, and may have some fears about the future. He is lucky in professions related to older people, ancestors, religious men wearing black clothing, and judges; accounting, construction, agriculture, mining, science, real estate, workmanship, mathematics, dentistry, historical writing, archaeology, astronomy, geology, engineering, and pharmacy.

Jupiter - Lot of Fortune

This is the most favorable configuration in terms of gains. The native may earn money without difficulty and his opportunities increase as he gets older. He attracts fortune due to his optimism and hopeful nature. He may be prone to exaggerated expenditures; he may even be extravagant. Jupiter brings opportunities through judges, senators, spiritual or religious people, lawyers, scientists, university students, government ministers, rich people, and through talents in education, finance, financial administration, politics, management, law, banking, spiritual and religious issues, astrology, and movies.

Mars - Lot of Fortune

This configuration brings opportunities and gains in competitive fields due to native's self-assertive and pioneering nature. However, he will also need to fight and take risks in seizing his opportunities and gains. Money doesn't grow on trees for him. He will benefit from brave people and situations which require courage and taking risks, and from professions related to physics, pharmacy, surgery, chemistry, iron and metal works, the production of explosives, security, the military, butchery, sports, veterinary medicine, engineering, carpentry, first aid, printing, or the tattoo business.

Sun - Lot of Fortune

This is one of the most favorable configurations for the Lot of Fortune, especially in a diurnal chart. The native's chances for recognition increase and he gets the support of powerful and influential people. He may obtain opportunities and gains through renowned, noble, influential, and generous people, and through professions involving management, medicine, politics, bureaucracy, acting, being the boss of his own business, trade, creative activities, precious stones and metals like gold, jewelry, or showmanship.

Venus - Lot of Fortune

This is a very favorable configuration. The native's profits increase due to his good relationships and cooperation with others. "If you love money, money loves you, too" is a valid approach for this configuration. It brings personal magnetism, good looks, harmony, and balance to the native. The native may benefit through women, artists, and mediators; he will be lucky in businesses involving music, plays, drapery, jewelry, dressmaking, singing, souvenir sales, women's apparel, and ornaments. This configuration brings a tendency to spend much money on luxury items and for pleasure.

Moon - Lot of Fortune

This is one of the most favorable configurations in a nocturnal chart. It increases the chance for gains. Her unfavorable aspects bring expenditures due to the native's unbalanced emotions. Being emotionally secure and earning money for his family are top priorities for the native. He is sensitive to those in need and he takes care of them. His opportunities come from women, his mother, social figures, and public services. He may earn money and gain opportunities through the food industry, religion, healing, hair care and styling, sales of silver and raw material, marine professions, public transportation, nursing, the service sector, lodging, homemaking and household management, and public relations.

Uranus - Lot of Fortune

The native may not enjoy stability in his financial situation. He may have ups and downs, and changing conditions. If well aspected, surprise profits may come, whereas if the Lot is unfavorably aspected unexpected losses may be experienced. There is a significant desire for financial freedom. The native prefers jobs where he may be comfortable and act freely. He is naturally creative, inventive, and original. This configuration also brings a potential to learn astrology. The native may make profit through scientific and technological issues, and things related to computers.

Neptune - Lot of Fortune

Although the native is not keen on financial issues, his opportunities increase when he does not push the limits and instead goes with the flow. He may disdain material things when they are needed, or make sacrifices in favor of others. On the other hand, due to his powerful intuition he knows where profit comes from, or he may profit through his intuition. He may be open to deception and abasement in financial issues. He is lucky in metaphysics, spiritual issues, marine and other activities connected with water.

Pluto - Lot of Fortune

Finance is one of the issues that brings crisis in the native's life. He may experience huge changes and transformations. He may have big ups and downs. He may need to fight to earn money. Favorable aspects may bring big profits and wealth. The native may be successful, have opportunities and prosperity due to professions related to investigation, criminal analysis, narcotics, and the discovery of secrets. Pluto's unfavorable aspects may indicate profits through illegal affairs and tyranny.

The Lot of Fortune does not only indicate our chances and gains in financial issues, but also indicates all fields and people that can bring us benefits: but they are earthly, not moral or spiritual issues. This is because the Lot of Fortune is also the Lot of the Moon, and the Moon signifies earthly needs and desires, what makes us happy, and what we are attached to. According to Robert Zoller: "In the natal figure, the part of fortune or lunar ascendant is a shadowy point pertaining to the emotional, instinctual, or inner motivation of the individual...[it] indicates the nature of the inner world of the individual and the quality and nature of its realization....[which] will [be realized] in the house wherein its ruler is placed. The success, failure, or history associated with this inner drive will be indicated by the nature and state of the lord of the sign in which the part of fortune falls. Moreover, the house in which the part of fortune falls will indicate the area of life which the native is emotionally concerned inwardly."[28]

In the coming chapter we will see interpretations for the Lot of Fortune in the signs, including in which fields the native will find

---

[28] Zoller 1989, p. 151.

opportunities and gain profit, and how he will feel lucky, happy, and emotionally completed. The sign where the Lot is located indicates issues which will bring happiness and pleasure to the native, as well as opportunities and profits. Moreover, the native's attitudes in using his opportunities and what motivates him may also be seen in these interpretations.

4: THE LOT OF FORTUNE IN THE SIGNS

Lot of Fortune in Aries

The native will be happy and successful due to his courage and creative efforts. Instead of waiting for opportunities, he needs to create his own opportunities and fight to obtain them. He may take advantage of ventures that others do not dare to, and be the first to do something. He may gain profits through management activities, politics, medicine, risky ventures which require courage, and speculative endeavors.

Lot of Fortune in Taurus

The native wants to obtain concrete results and stabilize his gains. He is peaceful when he is in pursuit of happiness and success, cautious and talented in pursuit of profits. Instead of risky and speculative ventures, he prefers taking sound and permanent steps in order to obtain opportunities and gains. He may gain profit through finance, and things related to land and nature.

Lot of Fortune in Gemini

The native uses his communication skills and talent in learning in pursuit of happiness, success, and gains. He needs to use his mental skills actively, to analyze opportunities wisely, to consult, to have an exchange of ideas, and to follow logical options while creating his opportunities. He may gain profits through literature, education, communication, sales and marketing, public relations, and travels.

Lot of Fortune in Cancer

The native may want to gain profits due to his desire for security for himself and his family. He follows his intuitions and is influenced by his feelings. Earning money through risky ventures is not suitable for him. For him, the key to happiness and success is security. He may gain profits through the home and decorative endeavors, landscaping, wining and dining, and real estate.

Lot of Fortune in Leo

The native's motivation to gain profits is to attain power, to reveal himself, and to have a higher status. He desires to earn well and to have a good life. Gaining an appreciation for other people motivates and energizes him. He is brave and courageous in creating opportunities for profits. He may gain profits through the arts, show business, and politics.

Lot of Fortune in Virgo

The native gives importance to being financially secure. His concern for the future is the most important factor in his efforts to earn money. He needs to scrutinize his opportunities and analyze all possibilities in detail. He uses his discriminatory talents to obtain happiness and success. He may gain profits through health and service sectors, and from endeavors which require sharp wit and an attention to detail.

Lot of Fortune in Libra

The native wants to have a peaceful and balanced life, and wants to share his life with someone he cares for. This is his main motivation for his earnings. He may make efforts to earn money and prestige for his partner or spouse. He is prone to making joint profits. He wants to earn money in a fair way and in the way he deserves. He may gain profits through artistic issues, decoration and aesthetics, law and justice, politics, and consulting.

Lot of Fortune in Scorpio

The native's motive for earning money is to find security for himself and his loved ones emotionally. He does not want to be offended and knows that money is power. While using his opportunities, he uses his intuitions rather than logic. To obtain his desires, he makes great effort and struggles a lot. He may gain profit through the military, medicine, politics, investigation, researches, mystical affairs, psychology, and psychiatry.

Lot of Fortune in Sagittarius

The native is in pursuit of freedom and power, which are his main motivations behind his desire for profits. He may want to travel all around the world, discover new things, and pursue the realities of life. He will find the happiness and success he desires, while running after his great hopes, or through his extensive mental abilities and by exploring philosophic horizons. He should be able take risks and maintain hope of profits. He may gain profits through law, philosophy, religious and spiritual matters, education, travel, publishing, and athletic activities.

Lot of Fortune in Capricorn

The native wants to be secure in his career and finances: these are his main motivations behind his desire for profits. He may have the happiness and success he desires through hard work, decisiveness, and reaching his targets. He may gain profits through management, social endeavors, organizations, governmental issues, and the positive sciences.

Lot of Fortune in Aquarius

The native wants to be mentally independent and to create new ideas. He may have the happiness and success he desires through useful contributions to others and new inventions. He may gain profits through academics, scientific issues and alternative sciences, and endeavors where he may use his creativity.

Lot of Fortune in Pisces

The native wants to make profits for others rather than himself due to his self-sacrificing nature. Instead of pursuing chances and opportunities, he waits for them to come to him. His intuitions are strong about where the profit comes from. His opportunities increase when he does not push limits and instead goes with the flow. He may have the happiness and success he desires by concentrating on higher ideals. He may gain profits through the arts, literature, religious and spiritual issues, and humanitarian causes.

5: THE LOT OF FORTUNE IN THE HOUSES

The house where the Lot of Fortune is located provides information on the fields of life the native will gain from, and on the amount of this profit. In traditional astrology, the house is more important than the sign it is in. If it is located in one of the strong houses, then the native effectively uses his opportunities and reaches a high level of welfare. I personally take it to mean that the native is lucky regarding the issues and people represented by the house, so that he may have profits in relation to them. Below you will see some interpretations for the Lot in the houses, showing where the native's opportunities, prosperity, gains, and profits will come from.

Lot of Fortune in the 1st house

The native is primarily a lucky person. Opportunities come his way. However, he also creates his own opportunities, especially when the Lot of Fortune is in one of the masculine signs. The native may make profit through his skills and outlook. He is his biggest opportunity. He is highly credible. This is also a favorable position in terms of being healthy and happy. The sign of the Lot in this house indicates the native's primary motives and emotional needs.

Lot of Fortune in the 2nd house

This position increases the native's opportunities for income. The native naturally knows how he will earn money. He may earn his living without needing others' help. He will be happy to earn his own money, or will earn through the things he is happy doing. The Lot in one of the financial houses may be a strong financial significator. Professions and people signified by the sign that the Lot is in, bring the native opportunities related to his earnings.

Lot of Fortune in the 3rd house

The native is lucky due to his siblings, relatives, neighbors, and other people in his close circle. Or, his chances come through these people, or he profits together with or through them. His siblings and relatives may be lucky and rich people. The native becomes happy when he shares his feelings and ideas with others and when he spends his time with loved ones. The native may profit from journeys, education, writing or speaking, and sharing his knowledge with others. He may be an author, teacher, or journalist.

Lot of Fortune in the 4th house

The field that the native is lucky in, is his family and home. He feels happy when he is secure in his home and family, or when he maintains his family's security. His chances may come from his family, and particularly from his father. He may also profit from real estate, landscape gardening, professions related to the land, or from a family business. He gets luckier in the later stages of life. He may be lucky due to his spouse, or his spouse may earn well.

Lot of Fortune in the 5th house

The native is lucky with his children and creativity. He may earn money from professions which reveal his creativity, either mentally or artistically. He may make income through his children. His children may be lucky. The native should take risks and profit from the stock market, games, sports, the arts, and the entertainment business.

Lot of Fortune in the 6th house

The native is lucky with his employers, assistants, and servants, or he may seize opportunities through these people. He may gain profits by serving others and also animals. He may be a doctor, nurse, or veterinarian. His employers, assistants, and servants may be lucky people.

Lot of Fortune in the 7th house

The native's spouse is his biggest opportunity, or he has a lucky spouse. His spouse, partner, or the people with whom he shares his life may be financially strong. He may gain profit through partnerships, legal cases, consulting, agencies, and public relations. Relationships, sharing life on a one-to-one basis, and acting together with others make him happy.

Lot of Fortune in the 8th house

The native's biggest chances come from his common resources with others, common profits, inheritances, and partnerships. He may gain profit through professions related to the skills or resources of other people, finance, banking and insurance sectors, and from accounting. He may get loans or credit to buy real estate or cars, and may profit from such ventures. He may also earn money from occult and mysterious subjects, psychology, and psychiatry.

Lot of Fortune in the 9th house

The native feels happy and earns money from distant places. He may gain profits through journeys, foreigners, the import-export business, and foreign places. He may also earn money from religious and philosophical subjects, spirituality, literature, writing, education, publishing, and research. Foreign people and distant relatives may bring him chances and opportunities.

Lot of Fortune in the 10ᵗʰ house

The native achieves success and happiness through his career. He easily finds jobs and earns money through his profession. He wants to have a high status and receive recognition in the outer world, and he is lucky in that. He receives the support of people in authority. He is lucky in governmental issues. His bosses and managers are also lucky people.

Lot of Fortune in the 11ᵗʰ house

The native is lucky in terms of his friends and people in his social circle, and he is happy when among them. He may be involved in charitable projects and feels complete as a result. His dreams may turn into reality and he may earn money from a business he always hoped to have. The financial conditions of his friends are good and these people help the native reach his ideals. He may earn well through his professional skills and his actions.

Lot of Fortune in the 12ᵗʰ house

The native has to work hard and push limits in order to grasp chances and opportunities, and he does it with some delay. He may not realize or see some of his opportunities. He may gain profit through behind-the-scenes activities, or working in confined places like hospitals, and earn his money by working in isolation. He may not like to show off his luck or income. This position may bring losses and bankruptcy in some periods of life.

6: SOME POINTS TO NOTE

In modern astrology, the Lot of Fortune may not be that important in a chart reading. However, it was a very important feature of traditional astrology, and was connected with many other issues. The Lot was not only related to the native's talents and the people who bring opportunities for financial gain, but also with the native's living conditions and quality of life. If the Lot of Fortune was favorably placed and not afflicted, and if its lord was well placed and not afflicted, supported by benefics, then the native would have a high standard of life and would live well.

The Lot of Fortune was also related to the native's length of life and his health, as the Lot is calculated using the degrees of the Sun and Moon, which are related to the native's general welfare. Since the time of Dorotheus and Ptolemy, the Lot of Fortune was known to be one of the main points used in calculating the longevity releaser or "hyleg."[29] If the Lot of Fortune is the releaser, then problems related to the native's health may occur during the hard transits of malefics (the conjunction, square, or opposition), or in progressions.[30] Since health is one of the important elements for happiness, the Lot (along with its house, sign, and aspects) helps us determine the issues which make the native happy. Money and opportunities are also important factors that make the native happy, since losing them brings unhappiness.

In addition to the house where the Lot of Fortune is placed, we may consider it as a kind of Ascendant and see where other planets are located relative to it: this was suggested by the ancient astrologers. For example, benefics located in the 11th house from the Lot

---

[29] **BD**: This is a point or planet which signifies the native's primary life force, used with timing techniques to predict longevity and other critical periods in life.

[30] **BD**: It was also used in primary directions.

of Fortune are very favorable. As the 2nd house from the natal 10th, the 11th indicates money earned by the native through his actions; just so, planets in the 11th from the Lot of Fortune are also important in terms of the native's earned income.

To understand the native's professional talents, we may consider the planets placed in the 10th house from the Lot of Fortune. Or, through the house or sign following the Lot of Fortune (its 2nd house), we may get information on matters which the native earns money from.

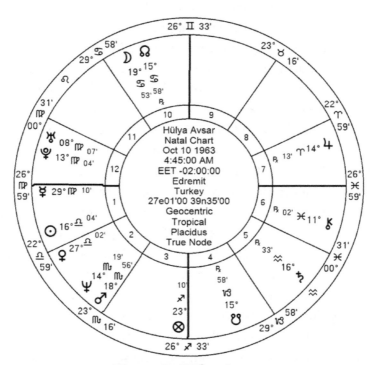

Figure 3: Hülya Avşar

Let's have a look at the chart of Hülya Avşar, one of the most popular actresses of Turkey.[31] The Lot of Fortune in her chart is in 23° Sagittarius, and in the 11th house (or rather, sign) from the Lot

---

[31] https://en.wikipedia.org/wiki/Hülya_Avşar.

is Venus, a benefic planet. Her Sun and Mercury in the 10th and 11th houses of her Lot of Fortune indicate her professional skills. Mercury in Virgo indicates her business mindset and her ability to make good plans in professional and profitable matters. Her Sun in the 11th house of the Lot, and his sextile with the Lot with a slight orb indicates she may get the support of influential and well-known people.

According to Schoener, to determine the native's financial situation, the elements mentioned below should be considered in turn:[32]

1. The cusp of the 2nd house.
2. The planets bodily in the 2nd.
3. The lord of the 2nd.
4. The Lot of Fortune and its lord.
5. The Lot of assets and its lord.
6. Jupiter.
7. The first two triplicity lords of the 2nd.
8. The luminary of the sect.
9. The lord of the Ascendant.
10. The first triplicity lord of the Ascendant.

Schoener also suggests[33] that we see whether "such a lord"[34] is in a cardinal, mutable, or fixed sign. If in a cardinal one, the native will have wealth through his own labor, etc. He also suggests we see whether the lord of the 2nd house is one of the superior planets, because in that case the native will also get assets from princes and lords: for the houses of the superior planets are houses of kings and princes.

---

[32] Schoener, Ch. I.9, **36-71**.

[33] Schoener, Ch. I.9, **73-74**.

[34] **BD:** In Schoener this is the lord of the second house, but perhaps he would extend this to other lords.

7: ANALYZING THE 2ND HOUSE

According to al-Qabīsī, the second house is "the place of property, livelihood and helpers";[35] according to Abraham ibn Ezra it "denotes money and possessions, and trading, and food."[36] In general, the planets located in the 2nd house, or the lord of the 2nd house, indicate how the native earns money, the resources and strength of his income, or how he may preserve his earnings. So, the lord of the 2nd has great importance, insofar as the native's income stems from professions of the nature of this planet.

Saturn in or as the lord of the 2nd house

Traditionally, it is possible to obtain success and wealth through working hard and making effort. The native may have taken on the responsibility of earning his income in the early years of his life. He is cautious and careful in spending his money and in making investments. He is afraid of being penniless in his later age and takes steps to achieve financial security for the future. He may be tight-fisted sometimes. However, this is conditioned by the sign Saturn is in. For example, if Saturn is in Leo or Aries (that is, in his detriment or fall), the native may experience unexpected expenditures. Saturn in this house or as the lord of this house may indicate gaining profits through construction, finance, or the accounting sector, or through labor, industry, and technology-related businesses.

Jupiter in or as the lord of the 2nd house

Obtaining wealth through decisiveness and success is possible. Profits may be used for noble causes and spiritual ideals. It is an

---

[35] Al-Qabīsī, Ch. I.58, p. 51.
[36] Ibn Ezra, p. 86.

advantageous position for earning money. However, if Jupiter is in detriment or fall, the native may have difficulty saving his money. Jupiter in Cancer (in his exaltation) is an advantageous position in terms of earnings. When in Sagittarius, he brings the tendency to spend a lot and be over-generous. When Jupiter is in Pisces the native may need money to provide security. Jupiter in this house, or as the lord of this house, may indicate gaining profits through religious, spiritual, or philosophical issues, from management positions, legal and educational issues, publishing, international issues or foreign trade, finance, and financial administration.

Mars in or as the lord of the 2nd house

Much of the native's energy and strength is focused on earning money. However, Mars in this position rarely brings a permanent profit as Mars is generally prone to consume. So when Mars is in Aries, although the native earns well, he also spends a lot. When in Scorpio, the native may preserve his savings. He may take risks in financial and business issues. He is strong in negotiation in monetary issues, especially if Mars is in his dignity. However, if in detriment then the native cannot preserve his earnings. Mars's placement here indicates the efforts that the native has to make. Mars in this house, or as the lord of this house, may indicate gaining money through the military, policing, firefighting, medicine (especially in surgical matters), the iron or steel industry, in chemistry and alchemy, and from businesses that use sharp tools and which require a high temperature.

The Sun in or as the lord of the 2nd house

The native may try to obtain power and stature through his wealth; he may have the support of respectable people. He is generally fair and honest in financial matters. When the Sun is located in one of the earthy signs, the native may be highly materialistic. When in one of the fiery signs, the native may either be generous and helpful, or use money to obtain power and display vanity. The Sun in this house or as the lord of this house may indicate gaining money through executive actions, popularity, governmental matters, strong people, people from the upper classes, politics, medicine, the sales of precious metals like gold, artistic activities, and show business.

Venus in or as the lord of the 2nd house

The native likes luxurious items that money can buy, and enjoys spending money on his pleasures and social life. His financial success comes from the beauty and fashion industry, or the entertainment sector. Venus in this house or as the lord of this house may indicate gaining profit through arts, politics, matters related to children, businesses related to women, clothing, ornaments, and souvenirs.

Mercury in or as the lord of the 2nd house

The native is successful in trade. He may also be successful in banking, communication, publishing, journeys, transportation, and the accounting sector. Mercury in this house or as the lord of this house may indicate gaining profits through his writing and speaking skills, his talent in interpretation, business life and trade, astrology and scientific subjects, publishing, and educational sectors.

The Moon in or as the lord of the 2nd house

The native may try to provide his emotional security through financial security. On the other hand, he may have some ups and downs in his financial situation. He is emotionally attached to his possessions and things from his past. He may obtain financial advantages through his family, his mother and other women in his life, or the public arena. The Moon in this house or as the lord of this house may indicate gaining profits through the food-related

professions, family issues, professions relating to women, transportation, communication, affairs related to waters and liquids,
retail, nursing, and public relations.

Uranus in the 2ⁿᵈ house

The native's finances may be changeable, with ups and downs. He
may earn money through his creativity and inventiveness, or he
may have unexpected spending. The native may find original ways
of earning and spending money. His financial relations are generally prone to imbalance and sudden changes. His relationship with
money is also unbalanced. He may spend carelessly and wastefully
one day, then penny-pinch the next. He may gain profits through
science, technology, electronics, discoveries or unusual or original
talents, astrology, or similar extraordinary fields.

Neptune in the 2ⁿᵈ house

This position which indicates possessions and monetary issues is
not a favorable one for Neptune, which is the planet of spirituality
and imagination. We need to give up the things related to where
Neptune is placed in our natal charts. Here, we need to go beyond
our ego. The native's attitude towards wealth may be unreal and
idealistic. He may experience disappointments, deception, and
illusions. On the positive side, the native may gain profits through
his imagination, inspiration, intuition, and his ability to predict
future trends.

Pluto in the 2ⁿᵈ house

Pluto is more suitable for the theme of this house than Uranus and
Neptune, due to its power. However, the native may have a
passionate bond to money and other valued things, and may not
easily give them up. He may strongly believe that money is power.
He may manipulate financial matters and the values he has. He
may be assertive or oppressive and also get exposed to oppression

in these matters. On the positive side, he may earn a certain amount of money due to his strong intuition, charisma, and courage. He may gain profit through investigation, academics, psychology and psychiatry, and metaphysics.

You may find other detailed information in my book on professional significators about the relationship of the planets, houses, and signs to professions and earning money.

8: THE LORDS OF OTHER HOUSES IN THE 2ND HOUSE

The lords of the other houses being located in the 2nd house of the chart signify the relationship between the native's financial gains and the other people and issues in his or her life.

The lord of the 1st house in the 2nd house

This position indicates that the native wants to profit and make himself financially secure. If the lord is in its dignity, direct and fast, not burned, not afflicted by malefics but supported by benefics, then the native profits through his personal skills and ventures. If the lord is unfavorably placed and afflicted, then he may lose money and have many expenses. Or, he may not earn as much as expected.

The lord of the 2nd house in the 2nd house

This is one of the positions that indicates a good income. This is valid especially when the lord is in its domicile. It indicates that the native earns money through activities directly related to the management of money. Earning money is important for the native. If the lord is unfavorably placed and afflicted, then he may lose money and have many expenses. Or, he may not earn as much as expected.

The lord of the 3rd house in the 2nd house

His siblings and relatives are related to the native's earnings. They may jointly earn money and have common opportunities. The native may earn money through writing, speaking, education, journalism, journeys, communication, and transportation. If the lord is unfavorably placed and afflicted, then he may lose money and have many expenses. Or, he may not earn as much as expected.

The lord of the 4ᵗʰ house in the 2ⁿᵈ house

His family and especially his father are related to the native's earnings. He may gain profit through family business, real estate, working from home, or through the business of his spouse or partner. If the lord is unfavorably placed and afflicted, then he may lose money and have many expenses. Or, he may not earn as much as expected.

The lord of the 5ᵗʰ house in the 2ⁿᵈ house

His children, or the friends of his spouse, may be related to the native's earnings. The native may earn money through them, but if the significator is not favorably placed or afflicted then he may experience some losses. He may profit through sports activities, the entertainment sector, speculative financial instruments, games, hobbies, creative talents, real estate, and opportunities coming from his family. If the lord is unfavorably placed and afflicted, then he may lose money and have many expenses. Or, he may not earn as much as expected.

The lord of the 6ᵗʰ house in the 2ⁿᵈ house

His employers, assistants, and servants may be related to the native's earnings. If the lord is unfavorably placed and afflicted, then he may lose money due to health problems and the above-mentioned issues. Or, he may not earn as much as expected.

The lord of the 7ᵗʰ house in the 2ⁿᵈ house

His spouse, partners, or representatives may be related to the native's earnings. If the lord is favorably placed and supported by benefics, then the native may gain profits through consulting, law cases, open enemies, lawyers, doctors, and astrologers whom he consults on a one-to-one basis. If the lord is unfavorably placed and afflicted, then he may lose money and have many expenses due to these people or issues. Or, he may not earn as much as expected.

The lord of the 8th house in the 2nd house

People with whom the native shares joint resources may be related to his earnings. If the lord is favorably placed, not afflicted, and supported by benefics, then the native may gain profits through people who are involved in such relationships with him, accountants, insurers, inheritances, compensations, and the financial opportunities of his spouse. If the lord is unfavorably placed and afflicted, then he may lose money and have many expenses due to these people or issues. Or, he may not earn as much as expected.

The lord of the 9th house in the 2nd house

Foreign people, teachers, religious and spiritual people, and distant relatives may be related to the native's earnings. If the lord is favorably placed, not afflicted, and supported by benefics, then the native may gain profits through higher education, journeys, astrology, or similar scientific subjects. If the lord is unfavorably placed and afflicted, then he may lose money and have many expenses due to these people or issues. Or, he may not earn as much as expected.

The lord of the 10th house in the 2nd house

People in authority, managers, bosses, and people working for the government, his mother, or his in-laws may be related to the native's earnings. If the lord is favorably placed, not afflicted, and supported by benefics, then the native may gain profits through his professional skills, public affairs, through taking responsibility, and being productive. If the lord is unfavorably placed and afflicted, then he may lose money and have many expenses due to these people or issues. Or, he may not earn as much as expected.

The lord of the 11th house in the 2nd house

His friends, social groups, communities, clubs, and people in these environments may be related to the native's earnings. If the lord is favorably placed, not afflicted, and supported by benefics, then the native may gain profits through his social skills and through being loved in his social circle. If the lord is unfavorably placed and afflicted, then he may lose money and have many expenses due to these people or issues. Or, he may not earn as much as expected.

The lord of the 12th house in the 2nd house

People behind the scenes, the employees or servants of his spouse, or his siblings' profession and success may be related to the native's earnings. If the lord is favorably placed, not afflicted, and supported by benefics, then the native may gain profits through working in isolation, spiritual affairs, health and healing, and behind-the-scenes activities. If the lord is unfavorably placed and afflicted, then he may lose money and have many expenses due to these people or issues. He may have losses due to hidden enemies. Or, he may not earn as much as expected.

The zodiacal positions of the planets in the 2nd, their position relative to the Sun, and their direct or retrograde motion, should also be considered. Jupiter in the 2nd house is undoubtedly the best position for making profits. The Sun in a diurnal chart (and the Moon in a nocturnal chart) in the 2nd house is also favorable for earning money. Venus in the 2nd house is secondarily favorable, whereas Saturn and Mars in this house are considered unfavorable. The North Node in the 2nd house brings profits, whereas the South Node brings losses. The Lot of Fortune being located in the

2nd is also one of the best positions. We may also consider the same for the Lot of assets in this house.

Let's give some additional information on malefics in the 2nd house. Morin notes:

"However, a malefic even in good state, always grants things attended by imperfections, or through evil methods or in difficult ways, or with some accompanying misfortune, because of the malefic nature of the planet through which it is more prone to evil than to good. Whence it can be said that malefics in good celestial state in the fortunate houses are like dissonance in music that has been resolved to produce consonance.

"Finally, a malefic in an intermediate state neither grants nor takes away anything but only prevents the good from taking place, especially if its nature is contrary to the good, as would be the case with Saturn in the tenth house. Thus, Saturn in the second in only an intermediate state neither grants nor denies money but through parsimony and avarice conserves whatever is obtained; but Mars there shows the squandering of money through prodigality and foolish or useless expenditures."[37]

How shall we interpret it when there is both a benefic and a malefic in the 2nd house? Of course, we will interpret each planet by its own nature, but it is important to make an interpretation based on their energies when they are together. To see what traditional astrologers think about this issue, let's have a look at what Morin said:

---

[37] Morin, p. 45.

"... Jupiter signifies foresight and Mars daring, and if both are conjunct in the tenth house and in good celestial state, considerable authority and power acquired through that foresight and daring are indicated in the area of the profession. In the second house these planets would show money acquired through foresight and daring action, as well as extraordinary expenditures."[38]

When two planets are conjoined in the 2nd house, the one with a better zodiacal position (by dignity, position relative to the Sun, direct in motion, quick, and so on) rules! This planet is more dominant than the other, and if it is a benefic then benefic influences are more dominant. Moreover, when these planets will have an impact on the native's life is determined by their proximity to the house cusp. Based on the statements of Morin, if Jupiter is closer to the cusp of the 2nd house than Mars, the native experiences his impacts in the early years of his life, and the impacts of Mars in the later years of his life. If Mars were closer to the cusp, he first experiences Mars's nature and then Jupiter's.

---

[38] Morin, p. 83.

9: THE FINANCIAL SIGNIFICATOR IN THE HOUSES

To determine where the native's opportunities will come from and what they will be related to, we should consider the house where the financial significator (such as the lord of the 2nd house, Lot of Fortune or its lord) is located. Let's see what the authorities said about this subject:

Financial significator in the 1st house

Abu 'Ali:[39] The native will be an acquirer of money without labor and worry; and if it were received there, there will be the highest luckiness in the good, and especially if it were received by a benefic and lucky star appearing in an angle.

Bonatti:[40] The native is going to acquire assets from his own person, namely by his own industry, with little worry and little labor.

Schoener:[41] If made fortunate, especially received by the lord of the Ascendant, or by a planet which has many dignities in the Ascendant, it signifies that the native will profit easily, by reason of his own industry and labor. But if it were made unfortunate, not received, it signifies loss in this, and that he will be unfortunate in matters he is responsible for, through his own industry and labor.

Lilly:[42] Signifies wealth acquired by the native's proper industry.

---

[39] The following adapted quotations from al-Khayyāt are from *JN* Ch. 11.
[40] The following significations from Bonatti are from his Tr. IX.3, 2nd House, Ch. 5 (pp. 1,211-14).
[41] The following quotations from Schoener are from his Ch. I.9, **201-25**.
[42] The following adapted quotations from Lilly are from his *CA* III, pp. 557-59.

Financial significator in the 2nd house

Abu 'Ali: The acquisition and his means of livelihood will be from a known thing, nor will he heap up monies.

Bonatti: He will find it because of his own possessions and his own goods; and merchant dealings and other arts which are employed with money, and the like.

Schoener: Made fortunate in the second (and especially received), he will have profit by reason of commerce, and by reason of his own money, or according to the nature of the thing signified by the second house. If it were made unfortunate, loss and misfortune in the said things.

Lilly: It shows wealth and substance are necessary to support the life of man, and also household-stuff, gain procured by the native's own labor.

Financial significator in the 3rd house

Abu 'Ali: It portends the bad condition of the brothers, and their labor.

Bonatti: He will find it because of brothers or sisters, or neighbors not related to him, or short journeys, or because of his own relatives or relatives by marriage [who are] lesser than him in riches and power and likewise age, or who consider him their elder.

Schoener: He will acquire profit by reason of the things signified by the third house, by reason of brothers, sisters, or blood-relatives, or by reason of a Church matter, and what is like these. If it were made unfortunate in that same place, he will incur loss by reason of the same.

Lilly: Signifies brothers, sisters, kinsfolk, near neighbors, short journeys, hospitality, sudden news or novelties.

Financial significator in the 4th house

Abu 'Ali: It denotes the good standing of the parents, and the native's durability in that home in which he was born, and the goodness of his condition.

Bonatti: He will find it because of fathers, or uncles or fathers-in-law, or other ancestral blood-relatives older than him; or from the use of merchant activities pertaining to lands or houses, or things which are dug up from the ground; or perhaps he will find a treasure underground; or from the use of furnaces and the like.

Schoener: Made fortunate in the fourth, profit will come by reason of parents or predecessors, or by reason of cultivation of the land, planting trees, vineyards, the building of houses, or he will discover treasure, and so on. If it were made unfortunate, say the contrary.

Lilly: It has signification of the father, of lands, of patrimony, immovable goods, buildings, foundations, fields, pastures, villages, treasure hidden anywhere, all manner of mines, or profit out of the bowels of the earth, husbandry.

Financial significator in the 5th house

Abu 'Ali: He will have children, familiar to the king's palace, and he will have many goods.

Bonatti: He will acquire assets because of children, and magnates carrying out the affairs of the kings, or because of medium-length journeys, or because of banquets or drinks which are sold in taverns or like places; or because of games and the like.

Schoener: Made fortunate in the fifth, he will have benefit by reason of children, grants, or by reason of taverns, and so on. If it were made unfortunate, it signifies the contrary.

Lilly: Male and female children, gifts, curious apparel, banquets, plays, all pleasant things.

Financial significator in the 6th house

Abu 'Ali: It means the flight of slaves and the loss of animals, and he will be generous.

Bonatti: He will acquire it because of male and female slaves, or servants, or small animals which are not ridden.

Schoener: Made fortunate in the sixth, misfortune is not considered by reason of the house. But if it were in one of its dignities (of the major ones), direct and received, and safe from other impediments, he will profit by reason of slaves and servant-girls, or by reason of small animals, or by reason of the imprisoned, and so on. If made unfortunate, state the opposite.

Lilly: Anything which portends or signifies sorrow or care, hurts of the body or limbs, servants, small cattle, uncles and aunts on the father's side; sickness and medicine, bees, doves, geese, hens, swine.

Financial significator in the 7th house

Abu 'Ali: It portends the accumulation of things from something unjust, and the squandering of the same on women and contracts.

Bonatti: He will acquire it because of women, or partners or enemies.

Schoener: Made fortunate in the seventh, he will take profit by reason of a wife or women, or by reason of the partnership of associates, or uproars or lawsuits, and so on. If made unfortunate, it signifies misfortune in the said matters.

Lilly: Marriages, women, partnership, lawsuits, foreign affairs, public enemies, thefts, rapine, all manner of wars, *etc.*, seditions.

According to Morin: Money will come through marriage or conflicts.[43]

---

[43] Morin, p. 97.

Financial significator in the 8th house

Abu 'Ali: The native will acquire assets from inheritances and on the occasion of the dead, and he will be generous, nor will he care in what way he spends or earns.

Bonatti: He will find it because of the dowry of women or their goods, or the goods of partners or enemies, or because of someone's death, or goods which are inherited by the dead, or goods owned by a woman apart from her dowry.

Schoener: Made fortunate in the eighth it signifies benefit and profit by reason of women, or by reason of riches from the dead. If it were made unfortunate there, state the contrary.

Lilly: The death of people, the dowry of the wife, the estate of women, unexpected inheritances, poisons, deadly fears, legacies.

Financial significator in the 9th house

Abu 'Ali: He will be an acquirer of assets from journeys and on the occasion of religion, and he will not care about [anything] unless it is of things not present, and his business will be because of foreign travel and those traveling abroad.

Bonatti: He will acquire it because of religion or the religious, or because of long journeys like those which merchants and others travelling far tend to make, and the like.

Schoener: Made fortunate in the ninth, he will profit by reason of Church matters, or by reason of long journeys, so that he will go to market in distant parts. If it were made unfortunate, it signifies that he will spend, and have loss, by reason of long roads or by reason of Church matters.

Lilly: Religion or godliness, the sects of religion, dreams, long journeys or voyages, churchmen, and things pertaining to the church, letters, wisdom, science, learning, scholarship, embassies.

Morin: Money through profession and good repute.[44]

---

[44] Morin, p. 97.

Financial significator in the 10th house

Abu ʿAli: He will obtain assets from the king and because of his purposes, and he will live from thence.

Bonatti: He will acquire it because of a king, or a profession or magistracy or office or other lay dignity, like a generalship, or a civil authority, and the like.

Schoener: Made fortunate in the tenth, [it signifies] profit and riches from kings and lords, or because he will be the administrator of cities or fortresses. If it were made unfortunate, state the contrary.

Lilly: Government, kingdoms, or principalities, office, power, command, honor, public magistrates, public administrations in the commonwealth, trade, the several kinds of professions; it peculiarly denotes the mother, and the native's proper vocation.

Financial significator in the 11th house

Abu ʿAli: He will discover assets from friends and businessmen and lenders, or from wares.

Bonatti: He will find it because of friends or soldiers, or household members of the lord, or by means of business deals, or lending, and harvests; or he will acquire from an unexpected fortune coming to him, or even because of matters concerning which he has the hope of making money.

Schoener: Made fortunate in the eleventh, [it signifies] riches and profit by reason of his own friends, or by reason of barons and the councillors of the king, and so on. If made unfortunate, state misfortune for the same reason.

Lilly: The happy conclusion of any business, friendship, the support of friends, profit arising by office or preferment, hope, comfort, promotion by the commendation of friends.

Financial significator in the 12th house

Abu 'Ali: He will earn resources and monies from prisons and enemies, and from every low-class work, and by doing something shameful, and he will be a thief and plunderer.

Bonatti: He will acquire it because of prison or the incarcerated, like sometimes guards of the incarcerated tend to do, or one who has released the incarcerated from their prisons for the sake of making money; or because of hidden enemies, or large animals, or some low-class and detestable duty, or from thievery.

Schoener: Made fortunate in the twelfth (understanding his good fortune just as was stated about the sixth), it signifies that the native will have benefit by reason of enemies, especially hidden ones, or by reason of large animals, horses, cows, camels, and so on. If made unfortunate in the same place, state loss by reason of the aforesaid.

Lilly: This is Bad Spirit; it has the signification of sad events, is the house of sorrow, anguish of mind, affliction, labor, poverty, imprisonment, private enemies, impostors, greater cattle who are fierce and hard to be ruled, harlots, horses, cows, oxen, bulls.

Morin: The loss of finance through illness, exile or prison, enemies.[45]

---

[45] Morin, pp. 64-65.

10: PRIMARY ISSUES DISCUSSED IN FINANCES

Whether riches will be gotten lawfully or unlawfully

One of the issues considered by traditional astrologers is whether the native's income is legal or illegal. William Lilly suggests we should follow these four considerations when making a judgment:

> "First, from the nature of the significator, whether good or evil.
> "Secondly, from the nature of the sign he or they occupy.
> "Thirdly, from his or their being or not being combust.
> "Fourthly, from being retrograde or not retrograde, for accordingly he promises good or ill, warrantable or indirect means."[46]

In general, if the significator is benefic in nature then the native's income is legal; if it is malefic then it may be problematic. Then, we should consider if the significator is in its dignity, burned, or retrograde in motion. Let's see what Lilly further said:

> "When the benevolent planets are significators of riches, and do not partake in any evil aspect with the malevolent, than the native shall obtain riches by warrantable and lawful means, and not indirectly.

> "If the infortunes be significators, and have no correspondence with the benevolent, they pronounce the contrary; so do

---

[46] Lilly, *CA* III p. 561.

they also, when either retrograde, combust, peregrine, or otherwise much afflicted.

"If a benevolent planet be significator, yet posited in the essential dignities of infortunes, then the native will obtain an estate by direct or lawful courses, as also, by indirect and unlawful means; judge the same, if the benevolent planet be combust or retrograde.

"The same manner of judgment shall you give if a malevolent planet be significator of an estate, and placed in dignities of a fortune.

"If a malignant planet by nature is significator of wealth, and constituted in the dignities of the fortunes, and yet notwithstanding shall be retrograde or combust, because that then the evil is conduplicated, the native shall attain more of his estate by unlawful or indirect proceedings, than by lawful or warrantable.

"On the contrary, if a good planet be in the dignities of the infortunes, retrograde or combust, that man thrives more by unwarrantable means than otherwise...In all this judgment, determine according to the plurality of testimonies, wherein you must have some recourse to the aspects of the significators with other planets."[47]

---

[47] Lilly, *CA* III pp. 560-561.

Schoener gives more details. He says:[48]

"Consider the significator of riches: which if it were Saturn, well disposed and made fortunate, the native will acquire them justly and with a thoughtful mind, but however with some fraud and lying; if he were made unfortunate, he will acquire them unlawfully. If the significator of riches were in the houses of Saturn, he will acquire them by reason of apathy, and difficulty, and ancient things, with betrayal and a malign mind, or by reason of the rustics, slaves, servant-women, or men of advanced age, and low persons.

"If Jupiter, the significator of the native's riches, were well disposed, he will acquire them justly, with all fairness and rectitude; if he were unfortunate, you will diminish and relax [that] according to his malice. The significator of riches being in a place of Jupiter, he will acquire riches by reason of just matters and Church matters, and from all things in which there is respectability and religion, and he will have them by reason of nobles, and those greater than him, or by reason of sages, judges, bishops, and the native will have familiarity with these people.

"Mars made fortunate as the significator of riches, signifies the native will acquire them in some lawful manner, however with an admixture of fraud and diminished plunder; if made unfortunate, he will not have them lawfully but unjustly and malignly. If the said significator were in the houses of Mars, he will acquire riches by reason of plunder, sedition, and by reason of lawsuits, theft, or rapine.

"The Sun as the significator, well disposed, he will have [them] lawfully, in a great and reputed manner; if unfortunate, unlawfully, and this will be in the open, nor will he care

---

[48] Schoener, Ch. I.9, **227-40**.

much about the people who criticize him for that reason. If the said significator were in the place of the Sun, he will have riches by reason of rulership or some authority.

"Venus as the significator of riches, made unfortunate, he will acquire assets justly, and in a friendly way, with a benign mind and the most pleasant words; if unfortunate, the whole is corrupted. If the said signification was from the houses of Venus, the native will gather assets by reason of ladies,[49] music, having fun, or maintaining lodging-houses and taverns, in which the works of Venus are practiced.

"Mercury as the significator of riches, well disposed, the native will acquire riches lawfully and with a subtle mind, and industry; if he were made unfortunate he will acquire unlawfully, in many lying ways. If the said signification were in the houses of Mercury, he will acquire assets by reason of writing and the sciences, or from commerce, painting, or geometry.

"The Moon as the significator of riches, being fortunate, he will acquire lawfully and justly, with a bright[50] mind; if she were made unfortunate, state the opposite. If the said signification were in the places of the Moon, he will acquire assets by reason of travels and moving, and from matters in which there is sudden change (such as sailing, and so on)."

Great fortune and wealth?

The ancient astrologers give us interesting information related to the native's biggest gains and losses. I would like to offer some quotations from different authors in order to provide you some detail and explain the logic behind them. Schoener says:

---

[49] **BD**: That is, female authority figures (*dominarum*).
[50] **BD**: Or, "clear" (*clarus*).

"The Lot of Fortune being in the houses of the lucky planets and in a good place, if its lord looked at it from a good place and one of its own dignities, and the Moon is received by the lord of the second, signifies an abundance of riches, and even that many will be enriched by means of him."[51]

As mentioned before, aspects from the lord of the Lot of Fortune are very important. If the lord is in its dignity and aspects planets which are dignified, it indicates that the native's financial situation will be good. If the lord of the Lot and the planets it aspects are in fortunate and strong houses, then the native's financial chances are good. We have already mentioned that the Moon's position should also be considered in addition to the lord of the 2nd house, especially in nocturnal charts. If the Moon and the lord of the 2nd make a good aspect or if they are in reception, then the native earns well.

"If the lord of the second house went to the lord of the Ascendant, it signifies the native will attain riches from an unexpected thing, and will profit from a good direction, if those making [it] fortunate looked. If however those making [it] unfortunate looked, it signifies he will profit from thefts or from charging interest."[52]

The logic behind Schoener's statements is this: a fast-moving planet applies by aspect to a slower planet, which means that it directs its rays towards it. So if the applying planet is the lord of the 2nd, and it applies to the lord of the Ascendant, then financial benefits reach the native without too much effort and even through unexpected ways. And if it is a benefic or a well-positioned

---

[51] Schoener, Ch. I.9, **105**.
[52] Schoener, Ch. I.9, **107-08**.

planet, it probably brings greater wealth. On the other hand, if the lord of the 2nd (which signifies monetary issues), applies to a negative aspect with a malefic, the native may earn money through illegal means or charging interest. In my opinion, this may represent the losses and difficulties that the native experiences.

"If the lord of the first approached the lord of the second, the native will profit from his own industry, and he will always be focused on gaining these things. But the separation of the lord of the Ascendant from the lord of the second signifies the native will not care much about profit."[53]

As Schoener states, if the lord of the 1st applies by aspect to the lord of the 2nd, it indicates that the native may earn money through effort, since the native is motivated to earn money. On the other hand, if the lord of the 1st is separating from an aspect with the lord of the 2nd, the native is not focused on earning money.

In addition to the position of the lord of the 2nd, we may also consider the position of the lord of the sign where the lord of the 2nd is located. If the planet which receives the lord of the 2nd house makes good aspects with the benefics, then the native's wealth increases. Schoener says: "If the lord of the second was made fortunate, and the lord of the first unfortunate, the native will be ignorant about seeking riches, but nevertheless he will be rich. Yet the riches will not be useful to him (however much the lord of the second is made fortunate), unless the planetary receiver of the lord of the second house had the testimony of Jupiter or Venus; and if it was well disposed, it will increase the riches."[54]

---

[53] Schoener, Ch. I.9, **109-10**.
[54] Schoener, Ch. I.9, **111-12**.

The lord of the 2nd house located in the 1st house, or supporting the lord of the 1st through an aspect or reception, indicates that the native may earn money without making too much effort, especially when the lord of the 2nd house is powerful. Schoener notes: "The lord of the second house in the Ascendant, or if the lord of the second house gave its own power to the lord of the Ascendant, and it is not falling,[55] it signifies profit without labor; if to the contrary, say the contrary."[56]

I would like to mention Schoener's opinions on the Lot of commerce, because when this Lot and its lord are fortunate, being located in the 2nd house brings the native profits through trade. "The Lot of commerce by day and night is from Saturn to Mercury, and projected from the Ascendant; which if it were made fortunate and in the house of assets, or its lord having dignity in the house of assets, the native will profit from commerce."[57]

We frequently see information on financial significators which indicate wealth in Lilly and Schoener. They agree that the Moon being close to the Ascendant, positive aspects between the Sun and Moon, the Sun's and Moon's aspects with other planets, beneficial aspects or mutual reception between the Moon and Jupiter, all indicate wealth and good profits, especially if these significators are in the 1st or 2nd houses or their lords are in these houses. Here are some quotations on this point:

"If the luminaries are in the angles, and they would apply to planets in the angles, the native will remain in riches, as he was born. But if the luminaries were in the angles and would

---

[55] **BD**: That is, "cadent."

[56] Schoener, Ch. I.9, **161**.

[57] Schoener, Ch. I.9, **191**. **BD**: In the Arabic sources, this is a Lot of debt and loans: if the Lot is made unfortunate, in a bad place, etc., the native may lose money from debt and loans; but if fortunate, etc., he will not (and, I suspect, he will gain from it).

apply to falling planets, the native will use up the assets of [his] progenitors. Which if the luminaries would be falling and apply to planets in the angles, the native will be raised up from a humble place to a high one."[58]

"The Moon in the ascendant fortunate gives wealth and estimates all life long."[59]

"The Sun and the Moon in trine, the Sun then in his exaltation, neither of them unfortunated by Saturn or Mars, give ample testimonies of a large fortune."[60]

"Jupiter in the second and the Moon in the first, or Jupiter in the ascendant in his own dignities, and the Moon in the second in her dignities, promises wealth."[61]

Schoener also makes similar statements:

"The degree of the zodiac which co-rises with the Moon (if she[62] was made fortunate) signifies good for the whole time of life."[63]

"Jupiter in the root being angular, or in his own honor,[64] or if he had power in the Ascendant, or he looked at the Lot of Fortune, or he is the lord of the house of the Sun in the day

---

[58] Schoener, Ch. I.9, **192-94**.
[59] Lilly, *CA* III p. 554.
[60] Lilly, *CA* III p. 554.
[61] Lilly, *CA* III p. 554.
[62] **BD**: Reading for "it." This seems to mean that the degree indicates something good for the native when it is later activated by other techniques (such as directions or solar revolutions).
[63] Schoener, Ch. I.9, **143**.
[64] **BD**: That is, "exaltation."

(or the lord of the house of the Moon in the night), the native will not lack property in his life."[65]

Schoener's and Lilly's statements are similar to what Māshā'allāh stated centuries before. Māshā'allāh also states that the Moon, the lord of the Ascendant, their aspects and receptions with the Lot of Fortune, their house positions, and their aspects with Venus and Jupiter, are indicative of wealth and profits:

"Which if the Moon were received, and the lord of the Ascendant in a good place, he will live and will be honored, and will have many brothers; which if there were not reception there, it designates poverty."[66]

"If the Lot of Fortune were with the Moon, and she[67] aspected Venus in a nocturnal nativity (or Jupiter in a diurnal nativity), it designates height[68] and a life just like if the Lot of Fortune were in a good place."[69]

"Which if the lord of the Ascendant and the Moon were in the angles, and free from the malefics, they indicate he has riches, and more if they were received. But if the lord of the Ascendant will be joined to some one of the luminaries in its[70] own domicile or in the exaltation, or the luminaries joined themselves to the lord of the Ascendant, it designates him to be eminent in riches."[71]

---

[65] Schoener, Ch. I.9, **162**.
[66] Māshā'allāh, *On Nativities* §1.
[67] **BD**: I say "she," indicating the Moon, since the Lots do not cast rays.
[68] **BD**: That is, rank and social elevation.
[69] Māshā'allāh, *On Nativities* §1.
[70] **BD**: That is, if the luminary is in its own exaltation or domicile.
[71] Māshā'allāh, *On Nativities* §6.

"And if the Lot of Fortune and its lord [were] in an angle (namely in the east), and they looked at the Ascendant, it indicates him to be very wealthy; which if they were in the falling and bad places, it designates him to have detriment and more, unless the lords of the triplicity of the Ascendant look at the Ascendant. Which if they were in the [places] falling from the angles and were joined with benefics in angles, it designates him to have good before the detriment; if the lord of the Ascendant were falling and in its own detriment, and were joined with a planet which was in its own exaltation or in its own domicile, it designates he has good after the detriment."[72]

"He will not be a pauper, in whose nativity Jupiter had some testimony."[73]

"The Sun in a diurnal [nativity] and the Moon in a nocturnal one being in the house of a fortune (and especially Jupiter), with Jupiter in a good place and status relative to the Ascendant, with the lord of the second being safe from the infortunes, will give great riches to the native, and high status."[74]

"If Jupiter looks at the second or its lord, he will have assistance from men, from where he did not hope for it."[75]

---

[72] Māshā'allāh, *On Nativities* §6.
[73] Schoener, Ch. I.9, **182**.
[74] Schoener, Ch. I.9, **183**.
[75] Schoener, Ch. I.9, **190**.

Providing profits through others

Profits coming from or through other people are represented by the 8th house. According to Schoener, Jupiter or Saturn located in the 8th house may bring wealth through inheritances, but at older ages:

"If Jupiter, being the lord of the eighth house, was in the second or eleventh, made fortunate, the native will have assets by reason of the dead."[76]

"Saturn in the eighth in the day—if he was not the lord of the eighth—signifies many assets in old age, by reason of the dead."[77]

According to Schoener, the lord of the 8th house may seem to promise profit through inheritances, but it should also be in aspect with the lord of the Ascendant in order to actually promise it. Additionally, if the 8th house or its lord is afflicted, the native may incur losses due to his partner's death or similar things. If the lord of the 8th is in the 2nd, the native benefits from other people's money. These benefits may come from deceased people, a partner, or enemies:

"If the fortunes ruled the eighth, not looking at the lord of the Ascendant, they signify the assets of the dead, but without profit."[78]

"The eighth house or its lord being impeded, signify that the native will be affected by loss because of the death of some

---

[76] Schoener, Ch. I.9, **113**.
[77] Schoener, Ch. I.9, **116**.
[78] Schoener, Ch. I.9, **117**. **BD**: The word for "profit" here is *profectum*, which might also be translated as something like "advancement" or "success." That is, there will be assets, but they will not help much.

woman, whose dowry will be forced to be restored with loss."[79]

"The lord of the eighth being a fortune, in the second, signifies riches from the assets of the dead, enemies, and wives (and more strongly than that if it was not impeded, or if it had a dignity in that place)."[80]

When interpreting the conditions for profits coming from others' resources, Lilly draws attention to the planet(s) or Lot of Fortune in the 4th or 8th houses, and their relations with the lord of the Ascendant or benefics. Lilly says:

"Saturn in a diurnal geniture in the eighth, in aspect with either of the fortunes, the native obtains a fortune by the death of persons.

"If the lord of the eighth is fortunate in some of his essential dignities, and is placed in the tenth house, the native will have a good fortune, and acquire an estate by the deceased.

"When the lord of the Lot of Fortune is in the eighth, and the lord of the ascendant aspects him, wealth comes by dead folks."[81]

"Saturn made fortunate, looking benignly at the lord of the Ascendant (and more so if he was the lord of the fourth): paternal things will return to the native by inheritance."[82]

---

[79] Schoener, Ch. I.9, **131**.
[80] Schoener, Ch. I.9, **89**.
[81] Lilly, *CA* III p. 554.
[82] Schoener, Ch. I.9, **166**.

Several astrologers state that Sun-Jupiter aspects indicate good luck. According to Dorotheus, the Sun-Jupiter trine indicates good luck and but also wealth: "If Jupiter looked at the Sun from the triplicity, it indicates wealth and much good fortune, and children, marriage, and a life in [high] rank."[83]

Loss of wealth

In the books of traditional astrologers, you may find information on losses as well as profits. To understand the reasons for losses, it is recommended that you consider the houses of the financial significators and see if they are afflicted there. Schoener notes: "Loss in riches will come about for the native by means of the sign and house in which one of the significators of riches is made unfortunate: for it could happen that someone would have riches from one significator, and he is fortunate in the matters signified by the significator and by its place, but he will have loss or misfortune by reason of another thing."[84]

For example, let's assume that the financial significator is located in the house of siblings or partners. This indicates profits through siblings or partners. However, if this significator is somehow afflicted or in an incompatible aspect (square or opposition) with the Lot of Fortune or Lot of assets, and if its lord is harmed (through being burned, retrograde, or in hard aspects with malefics), then losses may be incurred instead of profits. Schoener says: "The Lot of assets even being in the angle of the seventh house, safe, will introduce many assets by reason of women and open enemies, but the opposition of its retrograde lord, signifies the squandering of these."[85] And "the significator of riches being in the seventh from its own house, or in the opposite of the lord of

---

[83] *Carmen* II.14, **15**.
[84] Schoener, Ch. I.9, **118**.
[85] Schoener, Ch. I.9, **121**.

the Ascendant, does not signify profit from what that house signifies, but rather loss and expenses."[86]

The house where the Lot of Fortune is located is also one of the areas in which the native is lucky and feels happy. But if the Lot is afflicted or in a bad placement, in addition to problems related to money the native may also experience unhappiness. Schoener notes: "The Lot of Fortune being harmed in the twelfth house signifies long misery."[87]

Both the lord of the 2nd house and the Lot of Fortune itself being badly positioned indicates financial difficulties unless the contrary is indicated by other significators. A square or opposition between the lord of the 2nd and the lord of the 1st may bring a loss of wealth and poverty if there is no reception between them. Negative aspects between them may indicate that the native incurs losses and suffers from poverty due to his own faults. Let's see what Schoener tells us about it:

"The lord of the second being burned, and the lord of the Lot of Fortune badly disposed, indicate extreme poverty."[88]

"The lord of the second house being in the opposite or square of <the lord of> the Ascendant, if they did not receive each other, or were contrary in nature: the native will be a destroyer of his own assets."[89]

"If the lord of the second is in any sign which is in an angle, but it itself is falling from the angles, the native will have a

---

[86] Schoener, Ch. I.9, **128**.
[87] Schoener, Ch. I.9, **127**.
[88] Schoener, Ch. I.9, **149**.
[89] Schoener, Ch. I.9, **150**.

reputation for being rich, but he will squander them and will be poor."[90]

"The lord of the Ascendant being well fortunate, and the lord of the second badly [disposed], signifies few riches, and he will be anxious in[91] attaining them."[92]

"The lord of the Ascendant in the second house, made unfortunate: he will destroy his assets by his own will."[93]

"If the lord of the Ascendant looks at the lord of assets, or its[94] house, or the Lot of Fortune, with a hostile aspect, he will destroy assets with his own hand."[95]

"The lord of the second separated from the lord of the Ascendant, signifies that the native will be very worried about riches, but will just barely have the whole of what he seeks or hopes for."[96]

"If the lord of the Ascendant applies to a retrograde lord of the second which is giving its power to it, the native will labor much, but when he would seem to come into a little bit of profit, it will be taken away from him with annoyance."[97]

---

[90] Schoener, Ch. I.9, **152**.
[91] **BD**: Or, "worried about" (*anxius in*).
[92] Schoener, Ch. I.9, **153**.
[93] Schoener, Ch. I.9, **155**.
[94] **BD**: I take this to be the second, but it may mean the Ascendant itself ("its *own* house").
[95] Schoener, Ch. I.9, **163**.
[96] Schoener, Ch. I.9, **172**. **BD**: In al-Rijāl (which this is taken from), the native will be worried but will hardly apply himself to getting the wealth he hopes for.
[97] Schoener, Ch. I.9, **173**.

"If a retrograde lord of the Ascendant would apply to the lord of the second, rendering its own power to it, many paths of profiting would be opened for the native, but on account of his sluggishness, he will not get anything."[98]

"If riches are signified on account of the complexion of the lord of the Ascendant and the lord of the second, and the lord of the Ascendant is strong but the lord the second weak, the native will be much fatigued in seeking [them], but will earn nothing or little. And on the contrary, if the lord of the Ascendant were weak but the lord of the second strong, howev-however lazy the native is, he will have much wealth."[99]

It is important to know which planet is the lord of the 2nd house. Jupiter as the lord brings ease in making profits, whereas Saturn or Mars require making effort even if they are well positioned. Schoener says: "The lord of the second in the concealed[100] place, signifies many riches, especially if it was Jupiter; if however it was Saturn or Mars, it will signify acquiring great assets, but with labors and pains."[101]

The house where the lord of the 2nd house is located, indicates when the native obtains profits. According to Schoener: "If the native is going to have riches, and the lord of the second was in the Ascendant, he will have it in infancy; if in the Midheaven, in adolescence; in the seventh, in old age."[102]

The prenatal New or Full Moon degree should also be considered for diurnal charts. The houses of these degrees are also impor-

---

[98] Schoener, Ch. I.9, **174**.

[99] Schoener, Ch. I.9, **179-80**.

[100] **BD**: In al-Rijāl (which this is taken from), this seems to mean on or around the IC.

[101] Schoener, Ch. I.9, **175**.

[102] Schoener, Ch. I.9, **176**.

tant. According to Schoener: "If the lord of the sign of the conjunction or opposition preceding the nativity were in the second house, the native will be unfortunate in acquiring assets."[103]

Signs of poverty

According to Lilly, "The Moon in conjunction with Saturn in any angle, though a king, he shall be reduced to poverty; the square or opposition of Saturn and the Moon destroys the estate. The infortunes in angles, and fortunes in succeedents, or the Moon combust, and her dispositor unfortunate, or the place of the conjunction or opposition [before birth] oppressed of the infortunes and they cadent, the lord thereof being an infortune, and strong, or Jupiter cadent, and his dispositor not potent, the native from a vast estate, shall come to great want; and so the contrary."[104]

Saturn's conjunctions or oppositions with Jupiter, the Sun, or the Moon are not considered positive in terms of native's earnings but are rather considered as a significator of losses and poverty. According to the ancients, negative aspects with the Sun may afflict opportunities coming from the native's father, whereas negative aspects with the Moon may afflict opportunities coming from the mother. Dorotheus says:

"If Saturn looked [down] at Jupiter from the square,[105] it will diminish him in his assets...."[106]

---

[103] Schoener, Ch. I.9, **189**.
[104] Lilly, *CA* III p. 554.
[105] **BD**: That is, Saturn in the tenth sign from Jupiter, "overcoming" him from the superior square.
[106] *Carmen* II.15, **2**.

"If Saturn looked at the Sun from the opposition without the aspect of Jupiter...[then] if his father died, [the native] will quickly undermine his assets...."[107]

"If Saturn was with the Sun [by conjunction] he will corrupt the assets of his father...."[108]

"If Saturn looked at the Moon from the opposition, it indicates the corruption of his mother's assets...."[109]

"If Saturn was with the Moon, then it will corrupt his mother's good and her work...[and he will have] a powerful decrease due to the assets of his mother...."[110]

---

[107] *Carmen* II.16, **10**.
[108] *Carmen* II.18, **4**.
[109] *Carmen* II.16, **14**.
[110] *Carmen* II.18, **9**.

11: GENERAL APPROACHES

The best aspects are those between the Sun and the Moon, and between Venus and Jupiter, especially when one of them is in conjunction with the Ascendant or is rising in the natal chart. On the other hand, unfavorable aspects between the Sun and the Moon may badly affect the native's investments.

According to traditional astrologers, if the Moon is afflicted by malefics overcoming her (that is, being in the tenth sign from her and so squaring her), then the native experiences failures in monetary matters, and he cannot compensate for them if Saturn is in the 10ᵗʰ house.

The impact of negative aspects with the financial significators may be mitigated by conjunctions or positive aspects with Venus or Jupiter. Mars in the 2ⁿᵈ house brings investments, but if he afflicts the Moon then the native may experience losses through fire, theft, or other problems. Mars or Saturn located in the 2ⁿᵈ or 10ᵗʰ houses are considered as unfavorable positions in terms of financial issues if they are not well aspected by benefics or one of the luminaries. If Mars or Saturn, being located in the 2ⁿᵈ house, afflicts the Moon and this position is not made easier by the favorable aspects of benefics, then the native will always deal with difficulties in his life. When Saturn, especially when in the 7ᵗʰ house, afflicts the Moon, it brings financial losses and bad results that should be avoided in relation to the partners.

Jupiter, the natural financial significator, being afflicted by Mars and Saturn simultaneously, brings losses due to bets. Saturn in square or in opposition to the Moon brings losses due to being over-generous, extravagant, and open-handed. Jupiter in the 8ᵗʰ house indicates that the native may gain profits through marriage and partnerships.

If Saturn is in a favorable aspect with Jupiter, then if Saturn is the lord of the 8ᵗʰ or located in the 8ᵗʰ, then the native receives gifts and inheritances. If Saturn under the same aspect is the lord of the 4th or located in the 4th, the native receives an inheritance. If Saturn is the lord of the 7th or Jupiter is in the 7th, it brings benefits and profits due to marriage or partnerships.

If Jupiter is afflicted by Saturn, then the native may have losses due to being deceived by the people who take care of his financials, his agents, or due to some legal disputes.

Planets in cadent houses generally limit the native's progress in life.

Robert Zoller adds that the house where the lord of the Ascendant is located and its relationship with the planets should be considered, to determine the fields that the native will make profit from.[111]

Schoener notes: "A fortune being made fortunate and strong, and well disposed, not impeded, signifies that the native will profit from those matters which are signified by the house in which it is, and he will have good fortune in them."[112] But if a significator is retrograde, "the money will be made manifest to the native, but he will not acquire it,"[113] and "this native will scatter and really lessen what he has acquired, so that little or nothing passes over to his advantage."[114]

As for the fixed, stars, they "give great gifts, and raise men up from poverty to the summit of riches, more so even than the seven planets do, but often their gifts come to an end in evil: understand this if they were in the degree of the Ascendant, or Midheaven, or with the luminaries or the Lot of Fortune."[115]

---

[111] Zoller, *Diploma* Lesson 13, pp. 15, 22.

[112] Schoener, Ch. I.9, **93**.

[113] Schoener, Ch. I.9, **86**.

[114] Schoener, Ch. I.9, **120**.

[115] Schoener, Ch. I.9, **103**. **BD**: This sentence is based on the eminence and prosperity rules for nativities, which among the Arabs and Persians was classified with the second house.

12: HOW DO I WORK?

It is best to determine the financial significator using the rules we have learned so far, and then make interpretations based on the general condition of the significator and its aspects. Although I follow the order suggested by Zoller, who taught me Bonatti's techniques, I believe all potential significators bring some profit to the native. What I mean is: even if we do not prefer something like the Lot of Fortune as the financial significator, it will still indicate somehow the field in which the native may gain profit, even if it is unfavorably placed or afflicted. Similarly, the lord of the 2nd house brings profits based on its nature as well as the nature of the sign and house it is in, even if it is afflicted—but the profit it brings may be less than expected and it may even bring losses at times.

In any case, when determining the financial significator I follow Zoller's path and so I have a look in turn at the Lot of Fortune, the Lot of assets, the planets in the 2nd, the lord of the 2nd, and Jupiter's position. I generally prefer one of these significators as the primary financial significator. However, if all of them are unfavorable, then I consider the Sun's position in a diurnal chart and the Moon's position in a nocturnal chart. I believe the Moon's position indicates the native's earning potential in both diurnal and nocturnal charts. If the Moon and Jupiter are both favorably placed and not afflicted, then the native earns well. If the majority of the possible financial significators in a chart are favorable, then I think that the native's financial situation of the native is generally fine.

In addition to what we have learned from the traditional astrologers and my teacher Zoller, I believe we should also consider the 10th house and its lord, as well as the professional significators, to determine the financial situation of the native: because the native's earnings will mostly come from his profession. Additionally we may also examine the 6th house and its lord, as this house is related to the native's talents in daily work, his working principles, his working environment, and his employers; they are all related to the native's income. The lord of the 6th also indicates what the native works for or what he serves.

As suggested by the traditional astrologers, I absolutely consider the position of the Lot of Fortune in the chart. If not the Lot itself, but its domicile lord is afflicted, then I consider its other lords. I also consider the planets that aspect the Lot, as they indicate possible earning potentials for the native. As suggested by Bonatti and Zoller, I also consider the position of lord of the Ascendant to determine what the native is focused on and how he reveals himself. I normally use the Placidus house system, but I also have a look at the whole-sign chart and get more information. Let me clarify all these factors with an example, once again using my own chart.

In my chart the Lot of Fortune is in the 3rd house and in Sagittarius. It indicates profits through education, publishing, foreigners and distant places, international relations, journeys, close relatives, and siblings. The 3rd house is also the house of students (the 9th is the house of teachers).

I have generated income from all these fields. I worked in our family store in the Grand Bazaar, which is among the most-visited tourist venues in all of Turkey (not just Istanbul). During the 20 years I worked there, most of our customers were foreigners. When I was in the wholesale business for women's bags, I exported them abroad. One of my sisters helped me financially to buy a house. I have always been lucky with my sisters. I currently earn money through education and publishing. My own books have been published since 2006, and I publish the books of both Turkish and foreign astrologers through the publishing house I opened in 2011. So, these are the fields I earn money from. My Lot of Fortune is not afflicted by malefics. According to the traditional rules, in order to be active a Lot should be aspected by one of its lords: Jupiter, its lord, is in opposition to the Lot, and the Sun (which is one of its triplicity lords) makes a sextile to it.

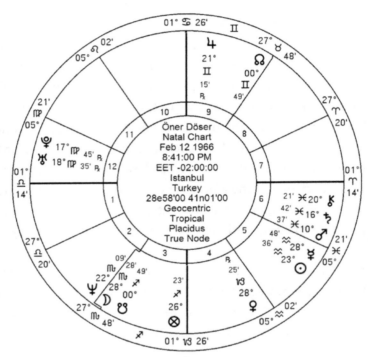

Figure 4: Öner Döşer

Then I consider the lords of the Lot, starting with the domicile lord. The domicile lord of the Lot is Jupiter in the 9th house in Gemini, and he is retrograde. Additionally, he makes a square with Saturn. Jupiter has three debilities: he is retrograde, in detriment in Gemini, afflicted by Saturn, and cadent. Jupiter's position here indicates the native's efforts in writing books and articles, teaching to masses of people who live in distant places, and expanding knowledge. However, great profit is not to be expected, but money will be spent for this purpose. This was really the fact for me. I have spent a lot of money for the translation and editing of my books and articles. I have attended seminars abroad and I still do. However, I did not earn much from all of this: in fact, what I earned was spent on my travel expenses. I also spent a lot of money for the transcription and translation of books which were written in Ottoman Turkish and Arabic, into Turkish and English. In fact, it was not my real purpose to earn much money. Instead, my goal has always been expanding my knowledge and sharing it in the international arena, and serving universal values (Jupiter is the lord of my 6th house).

So although Jupiter is afflicted, we may prefer it as the financial significator. Or, we may consider the other lords of the Lot of Fortune. There is no exalted lord in Sagittarius. Jupiter, the Sun, and Saturn have triplicity rulership, and the secondary triplicity lord the Sun makes an aspect with the Lot. In my chart, the Sun is in the 5th house in Aquarius. He is only afflicted by sign (he is in detriment), but does not have other debilities. Additionally, the Sun is in an eastern quadrant, is fast in motion, and makes a trine with the benefic Jupiter. The Sun is very favorably placed and his applying sextile to the Lot of Fortune makes him one of the possible financial significators. We also know that the Sun is involved in the formula of the Lot of Fortune. So, the Sun's aspect with the Lot indicates that the native may gain profits through professions like management and acting, through his father, or other masculine figures in his family, or through famous and prestigious people, or through making his mark and being famous.

The Sun in the 5th house also reminds us of performing acts and acting. According to Firmicus Maternus the 5th house is one of the places related to recognition.[116] These all work for me. I gained profits through my family, especially my father. I was also a business partner with him, which is signified by the Sun being the victor of the 7th house (partnerships). In my country I am known

---

[116] **BD**: See the numerous delineations to this effect in *Mathesis* III.

for my astrology education (3rd and 9th houses) and consulting (7th house). This is also signified by my Sun in Aquarius, his conjunction with Mercury (the lord of the 9th), and his trine with Jupiter in the 9th. My father was a famous actor in Turkey, very good at performing and talented in speaking. He also worked as a professional singer for five years. My talent in being on the stage comes from my father. This is signified by the Sun-Mercury conjunction in the 5th. (Additionally, Venus is in the house related to the father.) I have been the boss of my own business for many years. This is again related to my Sun and his aspect to the Moon in the 3rd (but in the 2nd house by whole signs), who is the lord of my 10th house.

The term and face lords of the Lot do not aspect the Lot, but Mercury does. This aspect explains my profits through education, writing, publishing, and trade businesses. As the lord of the 9th house, Mercury is directly related to astrology, teaching, publishing, and international trade. Its position in the 5th house also brings the chance to make profits through creative ideas and talent in being on the stage. Sagittarius, where the Lot of Fortune is located, indicates that I enjoy being involved in these areas of life, as I mentioned before.

When we erect the chart in whole signs the Moon is in the 2nd house, not in the 3rd as it is in Placidus. So, in whole signs the Moon becomes one of the possible financial significators. The position of the Moon is important in determining financial significators, especially in nocturnal charts. This is a nocturnal chart, the Moon is in the 2nd house and is lord of the 10th house. The Moon also makes a sextile with Venus, who rules the 1st house in both systems but also the 2nd Placidus house. All of these factors indicate that the Moon is an important financial significator for this chart.

Being in her fall in Scorpio, the Moon's powers are weakened, or this position indicates that financial opportunities will not be stable or sustainable. On the other hand, as the Moon has triplicity rulership in this sign, this impact is mitigated. The Moon is not afflicted by malefics, but supported by her sextile with Venus. Venus, being the lord of both the Ascendant and the 2nd, is related to me personally, my property and possessions; and being the lord of the 9th, she is also related to distant places, higher education, and foreigners.

When we consider that the Moon is placed in the 2nd whole-sign house, we may conclude that she is related to my financial situation as well as with my profession (since she is the lord of the 10th), and with distant places, foreigners, astrology, and journeys (as she is the exalted lord of the 9th). They indicate the fields in which I earn my living. Cancer in my 10th and the Moon in the 2nd indicate my earnings through our family business and my possessions and financial opportunities coming from my family. The Moon also represents the mother. Although I did not receive any inheritance after my mother's death, many years later I inherited some financial benefits after the death of her father; I paid for my house with the money I got after the sale of my grandfather's properties. So, the Moon is an important financial significator here and brings me profits due to her positive aspect with the lord of the Ascendant. Her separating aspect from the lord of the Ascendant may decrease the profits. In fact the Moon separates from her aspect with Venus but applies to an aspect with Mercury, indicating that I once earned money from Venusian businesses, but then started to earn money from Mercurial businesses.

In my chart Mercury is also the lord of Schoener's Lot of commerce (the Saturn-Mercury Lot mentioned above), which is at 13° Virgo. The Lot is also in conjunction with Uranus, the modern significator of astrology. Mercury is placed in Aquarius, an intellectual sign. Mercury is a secondary lord of the 9th house (as Gemini is intercepted in the 9th), which is also related to publishing and teaching.

As I mentioned before, we may also interpret the chart based on the position of the lord of the Ascendant. Quoting from Bonatti, Zoller says concerning the lord of the Ascendant placed in the 4th house: "He will be good, loved by his father and treated well by him and by his older relatives."[117] This was the case for me! I was loved and treated well by my father and his father. My grandfather decided to give me some of his stores in the Grand Bazaar, but I did not accept them and I provided for the fair distribution of his inheritance after his early death. I felt this was my biggest test and mission in life (the lord of the Ascendant Venus, in the 4th in Capricorn, the Lot of the releaser ("hyleg") or Lot of incarnation in the 4th). As a result, my family confirmed that I would work in one of these stores and not share its profits with the other family members. After I left the Grand Bazaar, I earned money from the rental income of this store and this money helped to support me and realize my goals in astrology. Since being at the Grand Bazaar, I now have an office in the real estate that belongs to my family where I give consultations and run the School of Astrology. Venus in the 4th house of my chart is also the lord of the 8th sign (8th house). So, I think the importance of the lord of the Ascendant in terms of finances is now clear.

Additionally, I consider if the lord of the 2nd house or another financial significator (the Lot of Fortune and its lord, the Lot of assets and its lord, Jupiter, and so on) is in contact with a fixed star. Fixed stars are more effective than the planets and may cause great fluctuations in finances as well as other issues. Let's look at the impact of fixed stars in Bill Gates' chart:

---

[117] Zoller, *Diploma* Lesson 13, p. 15 (see Bonatti, Tr. IX.3, 2nd House, Ch. 11, pp. 1,228-29).

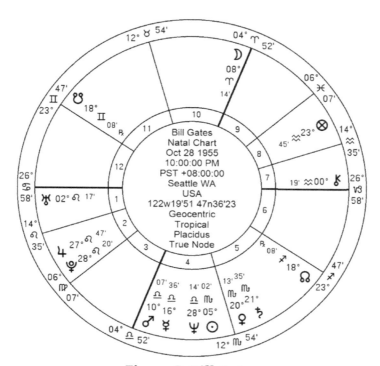

Figure 5: Bill Gates

Jupiter and Pluto in the 2nd house of this chart are conjoined with Regulus, a star related to great power. It is the strongest of the four royal fixed stars.[118] In this chart Jupiter, who is known as the greatest benefic and the universal significator of wealth, is in the 2nd house and in conjunction with Pluto, indicating a huge financial power. Jupiter in Leo is in his triplicity, and Pluto is in its exaltation. All of these factors indicate that the native will earn well. Additionally, Jupiter opposes the Lot of Fortune and so increases its strength. But what made Gates one of the richest men of the world is the Jupiter, Pluto, and Regulus conjunction in the 2nd house. Although Jupiter is afflicted by a square with Saturn, his conjunction with Regulus is a stronger factor than that affliction.

---

[118] **BD**: The others are Aldebaran, Antares, and Fomalhaut.

Jupiter as the lord of the 9th house, indicates the international and academic dimensions of his income; and as the lord of the 6th house, it indicates his relation to daily working life and employees.

Now, let's practice on other charts.

The example chart below belongs to a teacher (Figure 6). According to Bonatti, in analyzing the native's financial situation we should start with the Lot of Fortune. In this chart the Lot is favorably placed in the 4th house in Scorpio, together with Uranus. Its conjunction with Uranus may be problematic because it may bring ups and downs and unexpected losses. The Lot of Fortune in the 4th house indicates that the native may gain profits through his family, especially through his father and real estate. As it is placed in Scorpio, profits may come from fields like research, medicine, and finance. Mars, the lord of the Lot, is in a favorable position in Scorpio. This activates the earning potential of the Lot of Fortune. Mars in the 3rd house indicates that the native may gain profits through his siblings, close circle, education and communication, and short journeys.

The Lot of assets is in 14° Leo in the 12th house, but very close to the Ascendant. So, we may assume that it is in the 1st house. This position signifies that the native may make money through his personal skills (Ascendant) and his talents in management (Leo). The Sun, being the lord of the Lot, is in the 2nd house in Virgo and in conjunction with Mercury and Saturn. So, the native may earn money through the financial and banking sectors, editing, teaching, publishing, and management skills.

There are many planets in the 2nd house, which make this house a remarkable one. As stated in the ancient texts we referred to so far, we know that the planets in the 2nd and the position of the lord of the 2nd house indicate the native's financial situation and where he earns money from. All four planets located in this house are in Virgo. Mercury is the most dignified planet among them, and although he is burned, he is separating from being burned and will come out of the rays. Additionally, Mercury is the lord of the whole stellium here, and the financial victor according to al-Tabarī. So, Mercury is the best candidate for being the financial significator.

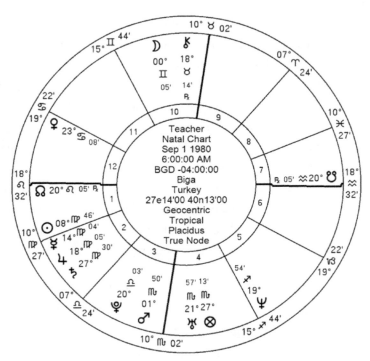

Figure 6: A teacher

Jupiter, who is the natural financial significator, is also in the 2nd house. This makes him a vital candidate for being the financial significator. But by being in detriment (which hinders him from being the financial significator), he is in conjunction with Saturn. These conditions weaken Jupiter's possibility of being the financial significator.

Among the four important significators we have analyzed so far, Mercury seems to be the strongest one. The native is an English teacher and earns his money through this profession. The Mercury-Jupiter conjunction and the Moon in Gemini in the house of the career (the 10th house) indicate this.

Let's study another example, once again the chart of Hülya Avşar, the Turkish celebrity. We start with Lot of Fortune. It is in 23° Sagittarius, in the 3rd house and close to the cusp of the 4th, and in the 4th according to whole signs. So, we may consider that the Lot is in an angular position. This position gives strength to the Lot and supports our decision in choosing it as the financial significator. The Lot conjoins Ras Alhague, a star which is related to healing and is neither malefic nor benefic. It is not afflicted by malefics and makes a sextile with Venus. Jupiter, the lord of the Lot, is in his triplicity in Aries and in an angular house (the 7th). He makes a trine with the Lot within 9°. Jupiter is not afflicted, but is only retrograde. All of these things indicate that we may regard the Lot as the financial significator. But we will take a step further and consider the Lot of assets.

The Lot of assets is at 21° Virgo and in the 12th house of the chart, but very close to the Ascendant. According to the whole sign system, it is in the 1st house. Mercury, the lord of the Lot, is strongly positioned and the Lot may be considered to be in conjunction with Mercury with some distance. The orb for Lots is 5°, but when they are close to conjunction in the same sign, I would consider this as a conjunction. In any case, the lord of the Lot is favorably placed and as a result we may consider the Lot of assets as a financial significator. But again we will take one step further and consider 2nd house.

Libra is on the cusp of the 2nd house and its lord Venus is located in her domicile. This is a strong placement! As a general rule, a planet in its domicile produces what it promises in relation to the issues of that house. Here Venus is not burned, but under the rays of the Sun. So, she is slightly afflicted. On the other hand, she is placed eastern of the Sun and moving fast, not afflicted by malefics and not supported by benefic Jupiter. So we may conclude that

Venus is favorably placed and we may also choose her as one of the financial significators.

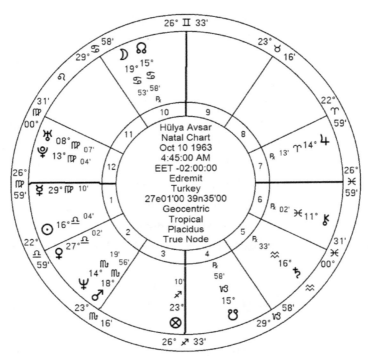

Figure 7: Hülya Avşar

Again, we will go further and consider Jupiter, the universal significator of wealth. Jupiter is in an angular house (the 7th) and in his triplicity (Aries). This a strong position. He is not afflicted by malefics, but is partially afflicted by being retrograde. He is not burned or under the rays of the Sun, which is a positive indication. Jupiter conjoins Alpheratz, a benefic star of the nature of Venus and Jupiter. So, Jupiter may also be the financial significator.

We have seen that all of these significators may be the financial significator. So, we may conclude that the native's financial situation will be fine. She will earn well in general. But, we need to determine a single financial significator.

I prefer Venus, because she is the lord of the 2nd house and also placed in this house. She is eastern, direct, and fast. There is no big problem for her apart from being under the rays of the Sun, but because she is separating from him she is gradually getting stronger. These are all positive indicators. Additionally, Venus makes a trine with the cusp of the 10th house, also a positive significator. She is eastern from the Sun, western from the Moon, and in contact with both of them (she conjoins the Sun, squares the Moon). Venus in her domicile and favorably positioned indicates that the native's profits will continue on an ongoing basis. Saturn, who is the exalted lord of Libra, is in his domicile in Aquarius and in a positive aspect with Venus. This means that Venus is supported by an important dispositor. Venus makes a sextile with the Lot of Fortune, so the native may earn money through the arts. The native once published a women's magazine in her name: Venus sextiles the Lot of Fortune in Sagittarius, which indicates that her Lot of Fortune is active and brings her profits. But its lord Jupiter is retrograde: the native stopped the magazine a few years later. The retrograde Jupiter in her 7th house brings her profits through her spouse and partnerships, but not as much as expected because she got divorced after a while. This means her Jupiter is working, but not with its otherwise expected performance.

While analyzing this chart, I would like to draw attention to the importance of the position of the Lot of Fortune in relation to the other planets. Below you may see her chart erected in the whole-sign system. Let's see what Bonatti says on this issue: "Also look at the eleventh sign from the sign which the Lot of Fortune is in: which, if some benefic were there, it signifies the honesty of the acquisition of the native's assets, and his good method of acquiring it. Which if one of the malefics were in it, it signifies the contrary: namely a dishonest method of acquiring it...."[119]

---

[119] Bonatti, Tr. IX.3, 2nd House, Ch. 12 (p. 1,231).

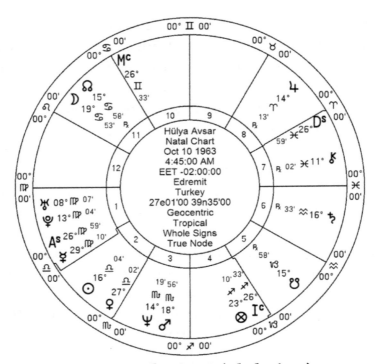

Figure 8: Hülya Avşar (whole signs)

Venus and the Sun are placed in the 11th house of the Lot of Fortune. As you may remember, Venus is the lord of the 2nd house: so she brings profits from arts. Her position in the 11th house of the Lot indicates that she will earn her money in legal ways and earn a fortune also. She was notable for paying higher taxes for many years and was the highest tax payer in Turkey in 2003. The Sun in the 11th house of the Lot of Fortune indicates reputation and earning money through being a personal brand. As mentioned before Mercury, who is the lord of her 1st and 10th houses, is placed in the 10th house of the Lot of Fortune and indicates she will be able to use her chances and opportunities in the best way, rising to a high status. His square with the Lot may bring losses, as she may refuse some profitable offers due to her occasional critical approach or perfectionism.

When will the native earn money?

There are a few techniques which could be used for determining when the native may earn money and make better profits. One of them is the triplicity lords technique, suggested by traditional astrologers, which may be used for long-term predictions because each period covers 25 or 30 years. The second technique is the *firdaria* method: the native earns money when the planet determined to be the financial significator becomes a *firdaria* lord. Another technique is profections, which may be used annually or monthly. As solar return charts go together with profections, we may see if the profits promised in the profection are also promised in the natal chart. Conjunctions, sextiles and trines with the financial significator in transits, secondary progressions, or primary directions may also indicate periods which bring good profits.

Working with the dispositors also helps us determine when the native will earn money. If the financial significator is favorably placed but its lord is not, the native first earns money but loses it over time and will not earn that well. If its lord is more favorably placed as compared with the financial significator, then the native may not earn well at first but he earns better in time.

If the financial significator is eastern, then the native gains profits at earlier ages; but if it is western, he gains profits at later ages. This is a method used in the timing of events which is also mentioned by Bonatti.

If the financial significator (or its lord) is retrograde, the native may gain profits in later years of life.

We may again study Hülya Avşar's chart, starting with the triplicity lords. It is a nocturnal chart, and the triplicity lords of Libra at the cusp of the 2nd house are Mercury, Saturn, and Jupiter (in order). We may make such an interpretation based on these findings: the native will make good money starting at an early age (due to Mercury's good condition), and achieves it through her own personal skills and physical appearance (the Ascendant). Saturn and Jupiter, which are the other triplicity lords, are in their dignities and powerful. So, the native will earn well at all stages of her life.

☽ Age 0-9	♂ Age 32-39	♀ Age 54-62
☽ ☽ Oct 10 1963	♂ ♂ Oct 09 1995	♀ ♀ Oct 09 2017
☽ ♄ Jan 21 1965	♂ ☉ Oct 09 1996	♀ ☿ Nov 30 2018
☽ ♃ May 06 1966	♂ ♀ Oct 09 1997	♀ ☽ Jan 22 2020
☽ ♂ Aug 18 1967	♂ ☿ Oct 09 1998	♀ ♄ Mar 14 2021
☽ ☉ Nov 30 1968	♂ ☽ Oct 09 1999	♀ ♃ May 05 2022
☽ ♀ Mar 15 1970	♂ ♄ Oct 09 2000	♀ ♂ Jun 27 2023
☽ ☿ Jun 27 1971	♂ ♃ Oct 09 2001	♀ ☉ Aug 17 2024
♄ Age 9-20	☊ Age 39-42	☿ Age 62-75
♄ ♄ Oct 09 1972	☊ Oct 09 2002	☿ ☿ Oct 09 2025
♄ ♃ May 06 1974		☿ ☽ Aug 18 2027
♄ ♂ Dec 01 1975	☋ Age 42-44	☿ ♄ Jun 26 2029
♄ ☉ Jun 27 1977	☋ Oct 09 2005	☿ ♃ May 06 2031
♄ ♀ Jan 22 1979		☿ ♂ Mar 14 2033
♄ ☿ Aug 18 1980	☉ Age 44-54	☿ ☉ Jan 21 2035
♄ ☽ Mar 15 1982	☉ ☉ Oct 09 2007	☿ ♀ Nov 30 2036
	☉ ♀ Mar 14 2009	
♃ Age 20-32	☉ ☿ Aug 18 2010	☽ Age 75-84
♃ ♃ Oct 10 1983	☉ ☽ Jan 22 2012	☽ ☽ Oct 09 2038
♃ ♂ Jun 27 1985	☉ ♄ Jun 26 2013	☽ ♄ Jan 21 2040
♃ ☉ Mar 15 1987	☉ ♃ Nov 30 2014	☽ ♃ May 05 2041
♃ ♀ Nov 30 1988	☉ ♂ May 05 2016	☽ ♂ Aug 18 2042
♃ ☿ Aug 18 1990		☽ ☉ Nov 30 2043
♃ ☽ May 05 1992		☽ ♀ Mar 14 2045
♃ ♄ Jan 21 1994		☽ ☿ Jun 26 2046

Figure 9: Firdaria periods of Hülya Avşar

Through the *firdaria* we may state that the native will earn well when Venus, the lord of the 2ⁿᵈ, is one of the *firdaria* lords. She may have earned well during the Venus-Jupiter period, Jupiter-Venus, and Jupiter-Mercury (November 30, 1988 – May 5, 1992). We may also expect profits during the Sun-Venus period (March 14, 2009 – August 18, 2010). She will be getting her best profits starting with the Venus period, which she will enter at age 54 (until age 62). Her profits will increase during the supportive transits that the period lords undergo. On the other hand, during difficult transits her profits will decrease or she will have difficulties in obtaining profits.

Through profections, of course she will reach her maximum profits during profections of the Ascendant to the 2nd house, when she is 25, 37, 49, 61, 73 (and so on) years old. She may also earn well during 9th house profections since that is ruled by Venus, when she is 20, 32, 44, 56, 68 (and so on) years old. The transits that Venus undergoes when she is the lord of the year may also give us information about how much she will earn.

Since Venus (who is the financial significator), is in her domicile, the native's profits will be continuously (but perhaps sometimes sporadically) well. Rising after the Sun (eastern), also increases her capacity and as she is not afflicted by malefics, the native will not experience financial losses and difficulties.

Appendix A: Table of Dignities

Table of Essential Dignities and Debilities (by zodiac sign), including rows for: Essential Debilities (Fall, Detriment), Domicile Rulership, Exaltation, Triplicity Rulers (Day, Night, Common — *Trigon Lords, Dorotheus*), Terms (*Bounds, Egyptian*), and Decanic Faces (*Chaldean*: 1. Decan [00° 00′ – 9° 59′], 2. Decan [10° 00′ – 19° 59′], 3. Decan [20° 00′ – 29° 59′]).

Appendix B: How to Calculate Victors

In traditional astrology, there are two ways of calculating a victor. One of them is to calculate the victor over a single zodiacal degree or significator in the chart. The other is to find out the victor over several degrees or significators.

The reason for calculating the victor over a single point is to find the most authoritative planet over that zodiacal degree. In other words, wherever a single significator (such as a planet or Lot) is located the victor over that degree is the planet which is the most influential over that significator. For any degree, the domicile or sign lord gets 5 points, the exalted lord 4, the triplicity lord 3, the term lord 2, and face ruler 1.

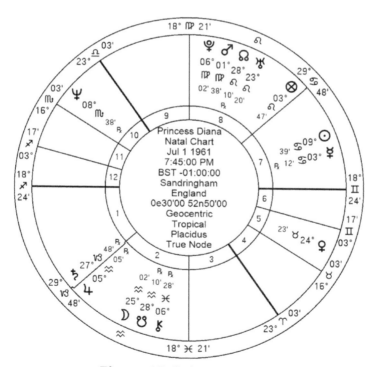

Figure 10: Princess Diana

The reason for finding a composite victor over several places is a little bit different: when some topic has several significators at once, the victor over all of them together is the planet which has the most to say about that subject. So if we are studying on marriage, we should calculate the victor over the following places: the degree of the 7th house cusp, the degree of its lord, any planet in the 7th, the Lot of marriage, the lord of the Lot, and Venus: we can do these one at a time and add up the scores for each ruler at the end, or do them all at once in a single, large table. The planet with the highest score is the victor and will have the most to say about the issues related to marriage.

Let's practice how to calculate victors using Princess Diana's chart, starting with the victor over her Ascendant (18° 24' Sagittarius). First, with the help of the table of dignities (Appendix A), the lord of the sign (Jupiter) gets 5 points. There is no exalted lord of Sagittarius, so no planet gets 4 points. Sagittarius is a fiery sign, and those signs have the Sun, Jupiter, and Saturn as their triplicity lords: each of them gets 3 points. The term ruler of the Ascendant is Mercury, who gets 2 points. The face lord is the Moon, who gets 1 point:

Jupiter: $5 + 3 = 8$
Sun: 3
Saturn: 3
Mercury: 2
Moon: 1

Jupiter has the highest score, so the victor over the degree of her Ascendant is Jupiter.

The composite victor uses the same method, but we need to calculate the victor over several degrees at once. Count up the points for the lords of each place separately, then then add up the totals: the planet with the highest score is the composite victor.

Appendix C: How to Find the Victor of the Chart

The victor of the chart is the key of the chart and the native's life; it represents the force that dominates the native's life. It may also be considered as describing the native's primary characteristics. To find victor of a chart, follow the steps below:

1. Prepare a table in which you record which planets have rulerships over the following places: the degrees of the Sun, Moon, Ascendant, Lot of Fortune, and the SAN (the pre-natal New or Full Moon) before birth. The domicile or sign lord of each of these places gets 5 points, the exalted lord 4, the triplicity lords 3, the term lord 2, and face ruler 1.

2. Give each of the seven traditional planets points based on which house it is in:

House	1	10	7	4	11	5	2	9	8	3	12	6
Points	12	11	10	9	8	7	6	5	4	3	2	1

For example, if the Sun is in the 3rd house, he gets 3 points.

3. Assign 7 points to the ruler of the day on which the native was born.

4. Assign 6 points to the ruler of the hour in which the native was born.

Add up the points for each planet: the planet with the highest score is the victor of the chart.

Appendix D: How to Calculate Lots

Lots (formerly called "Arabic Parts") are chart positions which signify certain topics, and are derived from the positions of three other things (often, two planets and the Ascendant). In the older texts, the Lots were calculated by counting the degrees from the first position or planet, forward in the zodiac to the second one, and then projecting that same number of degrees and minutes from the third point (usually the Ascendant): where the counting stops, is the position of the Lot. The counting between the first two points was usually reversed for nocturnal charts. For example, the diurnal calculation for the Lot of Fortune is: from the Sun forward to the Moon, and project from the Ascendant. But by night, one counts from the Moon forward to the Sun, and projects from the Ascendant. (In some modern astrology texts, there is no reversal by night.)

To make the calculations precise, it is useful to convert the degrees of the three positions into absolute longitude (between 0° and 360°), and add and subtract those values. For example, let's assume we have a chart in which the Moon is at 28° 28' Scorpio, the Sun at 23° 36' Aquarius, and the Ascendant 1° 15' Libra. Now, let's calculate the Lot of Fortune using these three reference points:

Diurnal: ASC + Moon – Sun
Nocturnal: ASC + Sun – Moon

Since the chart is nocturnal, we use the nocturnal formula. But first we must convert the longitudes of the luminaries and the Ascendant to absolute longitudes by adding the degrees of the beginning of their signs, then perform the calculation, and finally convert the result back into zodiacal degrees:

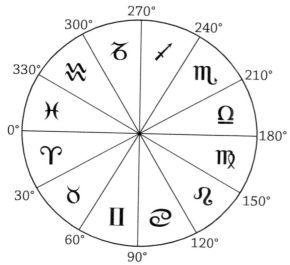

For example, the Ascendant is at 1° 15' Libra, which is 1° 15' more than the beginning of Libra (180°): so after adding the 180°, can say the Ascendant is at 181° 15'. (We can add 360° to eliminate sums that are negative, or subtract it for those over 360°).

ASC: 181° 15'
+ Sun: 323° 36'
- Moon: 238° 28'
266° 23' = **26° 23' Sagittarius**

See my chart in Figure 4 to verify this result.

Appendix E: Glossary

Accidental Benefic: A malefic planet located in one of the benefic houses; in dignity and not afflicted; bringing limited benefit but no affliction at all.

Accidental Dignity: The strength a planet gains for some reason other than its zodiacal position. Planets located in the angular houses fulfill 100% of their promises; planets located in the succeedent houses fulfill 50% of their promises, and planets in the cadent houses fulfill 25% of their promises.

Accidental Malefic: A benefic planet located in one of the malefic houses; in detriment, fall or afflicted; bringing affliction more than benefits.

Afflicted; Impeded: An indicator of weakness. It means being restricted, disabled and ill. Afflicted planets cannot fulfill their promises. States that afflict the planets are described in detail in Bonatti's *146 Considerations*. The most important afflictions are being located in cadent houses, being burned, retrograde, and being in conjunction, square, or opposition with malefics without reception.

Alcocoden: See **House-master**.

Alien: A planet having no essential dignities. Often called "peregrine." Such a planet is similar to a foreigner who travels in a foreign country and who has no rights or no business there. Its state in this position is linked with the ruler of this place.

Almutem Figuris: See **Victor of the chart**.

Almuten: See **Victor**.

Analogy: The similarity/ parallelism of the nature of the planets with the houses and signs they are in.

Anaretic: Derived from Greek; refers to a point that is fatal and destroying in primary directions.

Angles: The main structural keys of the chart, which give the primary house themes and planetary strength. Planets located in the angular houses have stronger and more visible impacts.

Angular Houses: see **Cardinal Houses.**

Aphelion: The point in the orbit of a planet where it is farthest from the Sun.

Aphetic: Refers to places which are suitable for the longevity **releaser** or "hyleg" to be in.

Arabic Parts: See **Lots.**

Ascendant: The degree of the zodiac which crosses the eastern horizon, and in quadrant house systems the cusp of the 1st house. The sign to which this degree belongs, is the "rising sign."

Aspects: From words that mean "to look at," configurations between two places in the zodiac which give information about how planets especially express their influences. on how the planets express their influences. The six "Ptolemaic" aspects are at intervals of 60°, 90°, 120°, and 180°. The conjunction is usually included among these, although it is not an aspect.

Bad Houses: 6th, 8th, and 12th houses.

Bad Placement: Being placed in its detriment or fall, being cadent, or being in a conjunction or aspect with malefics.

Badly Disposed: Being placed in a weak house and being not dignified. Having incompatible aspects and no contact with its ruler also makes a planet badly disposed.

Being in dignity: A planet which has at least one of the major dignities (domicile, exaltation, triplicity, term and face rulerships) is in dignity. The most powerful dignities are domicile and exaltation rulerships.

Benefics, Benefic Planets: Benefics are planets that assist the native in a positive outcome without making too much effort, bring benefits, support, and balance him in a moderate way. Benefic planets are Jupiter, Venus and the Sun. The waxing Moon and in some cases Mercury may also be considered benefics.

Besieged, Enclosure: A planet which lies between two planets (especially the malefics). A planet may be besieged through a conjunction or an aspect.

Burned: A planet which is 8.5° close to the Sun. A burned planet is afflicted. It is one of the debilities. According to ancient astrologers, it is the most serious debility.

Cadent Houses: 3rd, 6th, 9th, and 12th houses.

Cardinal Houses: 1st, 4th, 7th, and 10th houses. Also known as angular houses.

Cazimi: When a planet is within the 17' of the Sun, it is cazimi. A cazimi planet is "in the heart of the Sun" and so it is under some kind of divine protection as it is so close to the Sun's spirit.

Combust: See **Burned.**

Debility, debilitated: A planet located in the sign of its detriment or fall, where a planet is in the sign opposite the sign it rules (detriment) or is exalted (fall). Such planets cannot fulfill their promises. Malefics so debilitated cause trouble, so their malefic impacts increase. According to some astrologers, being placed in a weak house, having hard aspects with the malefics, being retrograde, and being burned are also debilities.

Declination: The angular distance of a planet north or south of the celestial equator.

Derived Houses: Houses counted from other places or houses, in order to see the chart from a broader perspective. For example, the 2nd natal house indicates the native's money; but because the 5th house is the 2nd from the 4th (indicating the father), the 5th house also indicates the father's money in addition to its normal signification for children.

Dignity: The strength, advantage, or virtue of a planet. This word is also used to describe the various types of rulerships a planet has.

Dispositor: A planet which rules the sign that another planet is located in. For example, if Venus is in Aries, she is disposed by Mars.

Diurnal Planets: Sun, Jupiter, and Saturn.

Domicile Rulership: If a planet is placed in a house that it rules, it feels as if it is at its own home. It displays its nature comfortably and fulfills its promises. For example, the Moon is the domicile ruler of Cancer.

Double-Bodied Signs: The mutable signs, which are Gemini, Virgo, Sagittarius, and Pisces.

Descendant: The point opposite the **Ascendant**, where the zodiac crosses the western horizon.

Duodecimae: See **Twelfth-parts.**

Eastern: Planets which rise before the Sun. Planets which are eastern of the Sun are powerful; they may fulfill their promises efficiently; acceptable and praiseworthy. According to the rules of medieval astrology, Mercury and Venus are eastern when they rise after the Sun.

Eastern Quarters: The quarters of the chart between the ASC-MC and DSC-IC.

Ecliptic: The plane defined by the Sun's motion, which the zodiac is centered on.

Electional Astrology: The branch of astrology used for choosing the right time for actions, often consulted for business ventures, surgical operations, signing agreements, buying and selling, etc.

Elevation; Elevated: A planet which is close to the Midheaven, even if having passed more than 5° beyond it. This placement indicates the things that the native prioritizes.

Essential Dignity: A dignity which a planet has through the zodiac (such as being in the sign of its exaltation). A planet located in one of these dignities have the power to fulfill its promises, but domicile and exaltation rulership are strongest.

Exaltation Rulership: A planet in its own exaltation is like a person who is near the king, who is respected and rewarded. Having exaltation rulership lets the nature of the planet be manifested plainly. For example: the Sun is the exalted ruler of Aries, and when in it he is "exalted."

Face: Each 10° of the zodiac: each sign has three faces, with 36 total in the zodiac. Each face is ruled by a planet: for example, the second face lord of Gemini is Mars. Although face rulership brings the least dignity, it is important anyway.

Feminine Planets: Moon, Venus, and sometimes Mercury

Final Dispositor: A final dispositor is a planet which all other planets are ultimately dependent on because it is the only one in its own sign of the zodiac (like the Sun in Leo).

Fixed Stars: Fixed stars for the constellations. Unlike the planets, fixed stars look stationary from the earth; but due to the precession of the equinoxes they move less than 1' per year and 1° every 72 years. Those closest to the ecliptic, and the brightest, have distinguished importance.

Friendly Planets: Planets which are compatible with each other, having the same natures.

Good Houses: Houses except the 6th, 12th, and 8th houses.

Good Placement: Being placed in its dignity or in strong houses, well-aspected and contact with its ruler.

Halb: One of the minor dignities indicating that a planet will be more active and influential. In a diurnal chart, if a diurnal planet is above the horizon (or in a nocturnal chart below the horizon), then it is *halb*. In a nocturnal chart, if a nocturnal planet is above the horizon (or in a diurnal chart below the horizon(, then it is *halb*.

Hayz: From the Arabic word *hayyiz* which means "domain": a minor dignity which is more influential than *halb*. In a diurnal chart, if a diurnal planet is above the horizon (or in a nocturnal chart below the horizon) and in one of the masculine signs, then it is in its *hayz* or domain. Similarly, in a nocturnal chart if a nocturnal planet is above the horizon (or in a diurnal chart below the horizon) and in one of the feminine signs, then it is in its *hayz* or domain.

Horary Astrology: A branch of astrology dealing with questions "of the hour." The astrologer erects the chart for the moment he understands the client's question, and makes a prediction. Horary astrology was widely used because people often did not know their exact birth time.

Hostile Planets: Planets which are incompatible with each other, having opposite natures.

House-master: Derived from a Persian word indicating a planet that grants years in longevity techniques.

Houses: The division of a chart into 12 sections, each of which signifies a particular realm of experience or life. The houses where the planets are located in a chart are important factors in reading.

Hyleg: See **Releaser**.

IC (Imum Coeli): The part of the zodiac passing the lower meridian to the north, and in quadrant houses the cusp of the 4th house. It is opposite the **MC**.

In contact: In aspect or conjunction with something.

Increasing in Light: The process by which the Moon's light increases until it is full.

Intercepted Sign: A sign which has no cusp on it.

Joys: Planets rejoice in the houses which are compatible with their natures and where they may express their natures comfortably. Planets have houses in which they rejoice (such as Venus in the 5th), and also signs (such as Venus in Taurus).

Local Determination: How a planet's general nature is specified to a particular area of life due to the house it is in. This phrase is a technical term in the work of Morin.

Lots: A position derived from the position of three other parts of a chart. Normally, the distance between two places is measured in zodiacal order from one to the other, and this distance is projected forward from some other place (usually the Ascendant): where the counting stops, is the Lot.

Luminaries: The Sun and the Moon.

Lunar Nodes: The points where the Moon intersects the plane of the ecliptic. The *South Node* is where the Moon crosses it into southern latitude, and the *North Node* where she crossed into northern latitude. Traditionally the *North Node* is considered to be equivalent to a benefic, whereas the *South Node* is equivalent to a malefic.

Malefics: A planet which requires a great effort to be productive, which brings trouble and restrictions. They are unproductive and prone to extremism. Planets malefic by nature are Saturn and

Mars. The waning Moon and in some cases Mercury may also be considered as malefics.

Masculine Planets: Sun, Saturn, Jupiter, Mars, and sometimes Mercury.

MC (Medium Coeli), Midheaven: Where the zodiac crosses the southern meridian, and in quadrant houses the cusp of the 10th house.

Minor Dignity: A dignity apart from the usual five essential dignities (for example, **hayz**).

Moiety: One-half of an **orb**, i.e. the number of degrees on either side of a planet or other point, which defines its special range of influence.

Mundane Astrology: The branch of astrology concerned with predictions for political, social, financial, religious, or military events.

Mutual Interaction: see **Mutual Reception**.

Mutual Reception: When two planets are placed in each other's domiciles, they are in mutual reception: they "host" each other. Bonatti suggested that these two planets should aspect each other for a mutual reception. On the other hand, Abū Ma'shar, Ibn Ezra and William Lilly suggested if these two planets are in each other's dignities by domicile, exaltation, or other rulerships, they do not need an aspect to create a mutual interaction: this is called "generosity."

Natal Astrology: The branch of astrology which casts a chart for someone's birth, with techniques for determining the native's personal potentials, tendencies, motivations, accidents that he may experience, financial situation, relationships, and so on.

Nocturnal Planets: Moon, Venus, and Mars.

North Node: See **Lunar Nodes**.

Ninth-parts: A subdivision of each sign into nine parts, each formed of 3° 20'.

Novenaria: See **Ninth-parts**.

Occidental: See **Western**.

Orb. A span of degrees on either side of a body or point, which indicates a range of power. See also **moiety**.

Oriental: See **Eastern**.

Paran: Star or star groups that fall upon angles at the same time that another significant constellation or planet is also upon the angles. They are viewed as attendants. In ancient astrology the term was also applied to the constellations that ascended with the zodiacal decans.

Peregrine: See **Alien**.

Perihelion: The point in the orbit of a planet where it is nearest to the Sun.

Powerful Planet: Refers to a planet's capacity to fulfill the things it represents naturally or accidentally. A powerful planet may have an impact on an end result. The power of a planet is determined through its position in the chart, including its essential and accidental placement and some other factors.

Primary Directions: A method of directions based on primary motion or the diurnal rotation of the heavens.

Quadruplicity: A qualitative division of the signs into three groups, each with four signs. These three groups are called cardinal, fixed and mutable signs. Aries, Cancer, Libra, and Capricorn are cardinal signs; Taurus, Leo, Scorpio, and Aquarius are fixed signs; Gemini, Virgo, Sagittarius, and Pisces are mutable signs.

Reception: When a planet host another planet in the sign which it rules. When two planets are in **mutual reception**, both of them gain power and they act as if they are in their own rulerships.

Releaser: A planet or point directed by **primary directions**, to predict the length of life and other life crises.

Retrograde: When a planet seems to slow down, stop, and turn backwards in the zodiac. It is one of the most important debilities. A retrograde significator is passive and has difficulty in fulfilling its promises.

SAN: See **Syzygy.**

Sect: A division of charts, planets, and signs into "diurnal/day" and "nocturnal/night." Charts are diurnal if the Sun is above the horizon, otherwise they are nocturnal.

Solar Arcs: A predictive technique in which each planet is directed at the same rate in which the Sun is directed in secondary progressions, with 1 year = 1 degree. There is no retrograde motion in this technique because it does not represent the native's psychology (as in progressions).

South Node: See **Lunar Nodes**.

Succeedent Houses: Houses which follows the angular houses: the 2nd, 5th, 8th, and 11th.

Syzygy: The pre-natal New or Full Moon degree. The syzygy before birth is used in many natal techniques, such as in predicting longevity or determining the **victor of the chart**.

Terms: A division of each sign into five parts; each term is ruled by a single planet. For example, Venus is the term ruler of Cancer between 7° – 13°. The luminaries do not rule any terms in the three standard sets of terms (which are the Egyptian, Chaldean, and Ptolemaic).

Tolerance: See **Orb.**

Triplicity Lords: A group of three planets ruling over each set of signs in a **triplicity**, divided into the day, night, and partnering rulers. Triplicity lords were used extensively by Dorotheus and later astrologers, to understand the support given to a particular point in the chart.

Triplicity: A classification of the signs into groups of three, by their elements: Fire, Earth, Air and Water signs. Aries, Leo, and Sagittarius are Fire signs; Taurus, Virgo, and Capricorn are Earth signs; Gemini, Libra, and Aquarius are Air signs; Cancer, Scorpio, and Pisces are Water signs.

Twelfth-parts: A division of each sign into twelve parts, each formed of 2° 30'.

Via Combusta ("Burned path"): The area between 15° Libra and 15° Scorpio. Considered to be a debilitating area, especially for the Moon. According to some astrologers like Māshā'allāh and al-Bīrūnī, it is between 19° Libra and 3° Scorpio, which are the degrees of the fall of the luminaries.

Victor: The planet which gets the highest score over one or more positions, according to the table of dignities; the most dignified planet of any specific zodiacal degree.

Victor of the chart: It is the key of the whole chart; the key for the native's life. It represents the force that dominates the native's life. It may also be considered as describing the primary characteristics of the native.

Void of Course: When a planet, especially the Moon, remains out of orb of any aspect (or does not complete an exact aspect) so long as it is in its current sign.

Weak Planet: A planet which has difficulties in fulfilling its natural and accidental promises, and cannot bring a result or cannot impact the final result. Weakness is determined through a planet's essential and accidental placement, along with other factors.

Well disposed: When the lord of the sign in which some planet is located, is in a good **zodiacal state**.

Western: Planets which set after the Sun. Planets which are western of the Sun have difficulty in fulfilling their promises. They have anti-social methods which may be questioned.

Western Quarters: The quarters of the chart between the MC-DSC and IC-ASC.

Whole Signs: The oldest system of assigning house topics. In this system, each sign is a house, so there are no intercepted signs. It was used by many astrologers, sometimes along with quadrant systems (such as Alchabitius semi-arcs, Placidus, etc.).

Zodiac: The belt of twelve signs.

Zodiacal State: A planet's strength (dignity) or weakness, especially in terms of the type of house, sign (dignity), and relationship to its lord.

References

Al-Khayyāt, Abū 'Ali, *The Judgments of Nativities*, trans. and ed. Benjamin N. Dykes, in Dykes 2009.

Al-Qabīsī, *The Introduction to Astrology*, eds. Charles Burnett, Keiji Yamamoto, Michio Yano (London and Turin: The Warburg Institute, 2004)

Al-Tabarī, 'Umar, *Three Books on Nativities*, trans. and ed. Benjamin N. Dykes, in Dykes 2010.

Bonatti, Guido, *The Book of Astronomy*, trans. and ed. Benjamin N. Dykes (Golden Valley, MN: The Cazimi Press, 2007)

Dorotheus of Sidon, *Carmen Astrologicum: The 'Umar al-Tabarī Translation*, trans. and ed. Benjamin N. Dykes (Minneapolis, MN: The Cazimi Press, 2017)

Dykes, Benjamin trans. and ed., *Works of Sahl & Māshā'allāh* (Golden Valley, MN: The Cazimi Press, 2008)

Dykes, Benjamin, trans. and ed., *Persian Nativities I: Māshā'allāh & Abū 'Ali* (Minneapolis, MN: The Cazimi Press, 2009)

Dykes, Benjamin, trans. and ed., *Persian Nativities II: 'Umar al-Tabarī & Abū Bakr* (Minneapolis, MN: The Cazimi Press, 2010)

Firmicus Maternus, *Mathesis*, trans. and ed. Benjamin N. Dykes (Minneapolis, MN: The Cazimi Press, forthcoming)

Ibn Ezra, Abraham, *The Beginning of Wisdom*, trans. Meira Epstein, ed. Robert Hand (Arhat Publications, 1998)

Lilly, William, *Christian Astrology*, ed. David R. Roell (Abingdon, MD: Astrology Center of America, 2004)

Māshā'allāh b. Atharī, *On Nativities*, trans. and ed. Benjamin N. Dykes, in Dykes 2008.

Morin, Jean-Baptiste, *The Morinus System of Horoscope Interpretation (Astrologia Gallica Book 21)*, trans. Richard S. Baldwin (Washington, DC: The American Federation of Astrologers, Inc., 1974)

Ptolemy, Claudius, *Tetrabiblos*, trans. F.E. Robbins (Cambridge and London: Harvard University Press, 1940)

Sahl b. Bishr, *On Nativities*, trans. and ed. Benjamin N. Dykes (Minneapolis, MN: The Cazimi Press, forthcoming).

Schoener, Johannes, *On the Judgments of Nativities*, trans. and ed. Benjamin N. Dykes (Minneapolis, MN: The Cazimi Press, forthcoming)

Zoller, Robert, *Diploma Course in Medieval Astrology* (Robert Zoller and New Library, Ltd., 2002).

Zoller, Robert, *The Arabic Parts in Astrology: A Lost Key to Prediction* (Rochester, VT: Inner Traditions International, 1989)

About the AstroArt Astrology School

Since its establishment in 2005, the AstroArt Astrology School aims at bringing sound and qualified astrological knowledge to society. In the constant pursuit of this goal over the past 13 years, it has succeeded in distinguishing itself and has been a pioneer in many areas, providing high standards of astrological education and creating a lively astrological community in Turkey.

The popularity of AstroArt derives mainly from our ability to offer a graded educational curriculum, covering both traditional and modern astrological techniques. We also offer many different specialty classes for those wishing to improve their knowledge after completing the certificate course. Our specialty courses cover a wide range of topics, namely: medical astrology, financial astrology, mundane astrology, esoteric astrology, Uranian astrology, cosmic astrology, horary astrology, and electional astrology. These classes are run by 11 different tutors who are expert in their chosen subjects.

We have also widened our teaching group with international lecturers, including Glenn Perry on astro-psychology and Aleksandar Imsiragic on Hermetic astrology. Gaye Döşer also presents on cosmic astrology and healing. We have also expanded our esoteric astrology studies by applying Islamic mysticism (Sufism) to astrology.

We are proud to have created many ways of providing knowledge on a country-wide basis: our online interactive classes and our web broadcasts through Astrology TV derive from this mission. So far we reach Germany, Holland, and Cyprus, as well as many other cities, by which we have brought a solid education to those who are physically unable to attend the school.

Our school also has been a pioneer in bringing its educational program into an internationally recognized Turkish university (Girne American University), and hence providing recognition with a certificate of acknowledgment for astrology education at the university level. Certificates are given and signed by the rectorate, and classes are held on university premises. This program started in 2014 and students should exhibit 75% eligibility in obtaining the certificate.

Apart from online web broadcasting, we have established our own publishing company to provide our own textbooks, and we have also liaised with international astrologers who provide their knowledge for Turkish readers, including **Glenn Perry, Lea Imsiragic, Deborah Houlding, and Benjamin Dykes.**

Our school is situated in Istanbul, which has been a bridge between Eastern and Western cultures for centuries. Hence, apart from teaching and distributing knowledge we have the vision to create an internationally recognized social environment for followers of astrology, sharing astrological developments on a worldwide scale. To that end, since 2012 we have organized the annual "International Astrology Days" in March at the spring equinox. Every year we provide a special discussion topic for our international guest speakers to elaborate on for the benefit of the public, in addition to seminars and workshops for astrology students. We publish the outcome as a separate volume.

International Astrology Days Activities in Istanbul (since 2012)

Our school is now a proud affiliate of ISAR (International Society for Astrological Research), through which it is now able to provide its students the opportunity to obtain an internationally recognized proficiency certificate for their astrology education. We believe that this is a great chance for students who want to enjoy a worldwide mutual understanding for their level of astrological knowledge, as well as being a member of a school whose name is amongst the top names of worldwide schools.

An ISAR-affiliated school offers advantages for expanding one's borders and liaise within a worldwide network which is constantly in tune with the current developments of astrological knowledge, as one of the prime purposes of the ISAR Affiliated School Program is to create an educational resource for astrologers worldwide. ISAR only recognizes those schools of astrology whose curriculum enables its students of astrology to acquire mutually accepted global standards of knowledge, contributing to a worldwide professional education.